HOW TO GO
NO-CONTACT
WITH YOUR
NARCISSISTIC MOTHER
Even though you think you can't

DANU MORRIGAN

DARTON · LONGMAN + TODD

Dedication

This book is dedicated to my wonderful David, and to their partner Bowe who is a joy in my life and who absolutely definitely isn't the worst.

And to all the wonderful DONMs I have been privileged to 'meet' all this time. Your courage and tenacity and kindness and compassion blows me away every time.

First published in 2024 by
Darton, Longman and Todd Ltd
Unit I, The Exchange
6 Scarbrook Road
Croydon CR0 IUH

© 2024 Danu Morrigan

The right of Danu Morrigan to be identified as the Author of this work
has been asserted in accordance with the Copyright, Designs and
Patents Act 1988.

ISBN: 978-1-915412-66-9

A catalogue record for this book is available from the British Library.

Printed and bound in Great Britain by Bell & Bain, Glasgow

Contents

Notes on Content
AI-FREE ZONE

I confirm that this whole book has been written by me, Danu Morrigan, without one word coming from AI. In this way it is really me, Danu, speaking to you as you go on this journey and not some machine.

Note on Spelling

As an Irishwoman I use the island version of English: i.e. the English we use in Ireland, Britain, Australia and New Zealand (and sometimes Canada?). So if you come across words like *neighbour*, *favour* and *labour*, that's why. Likewise words that in the U.S end in ~ize but we spell with an ~ise such as *realise*. And spellings like *centre* rather than *center*. We also say *practise* when it's a verb, saving *practice* for nouns only.

None of these are typos.

Note on Acronyms

I use the acronym DONM in this book, and it stands for Daughter Of a Narcissistic Mother.

Chapter 1
INTRODUCTION
AND WELCOME

1.1: Who is this book for?

If you are forever struggling in your relationship with your mother, if she is always hurting you, if you come away from every encounter emotionally bruised, and you'd love all that to stop but you can't think how, this book is for you.

If you understand that your mother is narcissistic and would love to cut off contact with her, but feel obliged to stay in contact with her, this book is for you.

If you feel guilty at even the thought of leaving your mother, this book is for you.

If you'd like to be empowered to make a decision about your future relationship with your mother, and make that decision in peace, strength and serenity, knowing how to manage your beliefs and feelings about that, and knowing the logistics of how to do it with the least pain and drama for all concerned, then this book is definitely for you.

You are not alone in your doubts and fears and stuckness, and there is a solution, and you're holding it in your hands right now.

Now, it's important to note that this book will not *make* you go No-Contact. It will enable you to make a true decision. The power always remains with you. The motto of this book is: 'Be Free', and after reading this book and doing its exercises, you will be.

1.2: Who am I?
And why should you listen to me?

This book is about you, not me, so I'll be brief, telling you only as much as you need to know in order to have confidence that I am the right person to share this information with you.

I am Danu Morrigan and in 2008 I realised that my mother was narcissistic. Best guess anyway, as she was never professionally diagnosed. But it explained everything about her behaviour, the relationship she and I had, and the fallout of it on my life.

This realisation started me on a journey I could never have imagined.

That same year I created the website www. daughtersofnarcissisticmothers.com to share information about narcissistic mothers and their impact on us, their daughters.

In 2012 my first book *You're Not Crazy – It's Your Mother* was published – as this book is – by Darton, Longman and Todd in the UK. This was followed by *Dear Daughter* and *To The Unloved Daughter.*

Since 2008 I have been in communication with thousands of DONMs, and over and over I have heard them say: 'I'd love to go No-Contact but ...' and after the 'but' came all their reasons.

My heart would break at these women trapped in these toxic relationships, and that is why I have written this book to help them – and you – to go No-Contact with your narcissistic mother even though you might be certain that you can't.

Because I know that you *can*, and in this book I show you *how*.

I also need to confirm that I am not a qualified anything with regard to psychology. I have been learning and researching all of this stuff since 2008, but I don't have any bits of paper, and I don't want to misrepresent myself.

1.3: The format of this book

This book is a mixture of information and exercises. The exercises are a mixture of writing, speaking and physical actions, and are all very easy. I do invite you to actually do the exercises as they are what will take the information in this book off the page and into your life. They're what will make it all real rather than theoretical.

To do the writing exercises you can use an ordinary notebook, or type them, or you can get my optional printables via donm.info/htgnc-resources. You'll find other information at that link too such as sources and citations.

And then we'll take a step-by-step approach, exploring why you might go No-Contact, reasons to stay in Contact that might apply to you, whether you should try one more time to fix things with your mother and how to go about it if so, and what to expect from it.

Then we spend a good bit of time discussing how it's our beliefs that tell us what we're allowed and not allowed to do, and we explore how accurate all of that is, and how to be the boss of our beliefs. We share amazing techniques to facilitate this, and you'll find these useful in the rest of your life too, not just for this topic.

Then we go through all your possible beliefs which stop you going No-Contact, and we work to resolve them all in favour of empowerment and accuracy.

And then we discuss all the logistics of going No-Contact, and how best to actually do it, followed by what fallout you might expect and how to manage it all, again, in power and peace.

1.4: A warning before we go further

Now, before we launch into the rest of this book, and to make sure you get full value from this information, I need to explain something first. It's this:

In a very real way we are all run by committee.

As Ralph Waldo Emerson said, 'I am large, I contain multitudes', and this applies to us all. What this means is that there is no single *You* who is operating your life. In a very real sense our life is run by various 'committee members'. You'll have experienced this any time you said something like, 'Well, part of me would love to do [the thing], but the other part is scared I'll mess it up.'

All works well when the committee members are in agreement, but often, as in our example above where you wanted to do the thing *and* you were nervous to do it, they have competing agendas.

Actually, that's not quite right. It's more accurate to say that every committee member has the same agenda, which is to keep you safe and happy. So they are all your friends; there are no bad guys here.

However, they might have different beliefs about the best way to keep you safe and happy, and that causes them to have different opinions about what you should do. So in our example one Committee Member wants to do the thing because it will add value to your life in some way, and another doesn't want you to do the thing because you might mess it up, and the implications of that including shame, embarrassment, loss, rejection and so on.

And we can say already – by the very fact that you are reading this book – that there are at least two committee members holding different opinions about the issue of going No-Contact.

There is the committee member who wants to go No-Contact:

This is the committee member who purchased this book, who is willing to invest the time to find out how to go No-Contact.

But then there is another committee member who has another point of view:

I know this committee member exists too, because if she didn't, you would have already gone No-Contact in peace, power, and serenity, and wouldn't need this information to help you do it.

In fact, the title of this book refers to both committee members: *How To Go No-Contact* refers to the one who wants No-Contact, and *Even Though You Think You Can't* refers to, well, the one who thinks you can't.

It is precisely because of this conflict that you need this book.

Now, the committee member who wants to go No-Contact has got her way so far, by allowing you to purchase this book and to start reading these very words.

But this will be extremely threatening for the committee member who thinks you cannot and should not go No-Contact.

Now I need to say that the *Stay-in-Contact* committee member has very good reasons for her opinion and we will be going into these reasons later in a lot of detail. Yes, with a view to resolving those reasons and helping her realise she doesn't have to keep to them, but not to dismiss those reasons. They are real, and valid, and appropriate. They're just not true.

And the *Stay-In-Contact* committee member will very possibly try to sabotage you (which is, in her mind, keeping you safe) from continuing with this book, so do watch out for that.

This committee member may know that it would be too challenging to the *Go-No-Contact-Committee-Member* to get you to abandon this book completely, but if they can get you to procrastinate indefinitely on doing it, then that creates the same result without having to force you to decide not to read on.

The tool the *Stay-In-Contact* committee member is most likely to use is *resistance*. You may find that as you plan to read and/or continue reading this book, you will find that your brain will come up with excuses why you should not do it, or at least not do it right now.

So I say to you – the You who wants to go No-Contact – to be aware of this risk and to be prepared to use willpower to override it. You won't have to use willpower indefinitely as a huge part of this book is about helping the *Stay-In-Contact* committee member realise that it's okay to go No-Contact. But, if you don't keep going through this resource, we'll never get to that stage. So this is a bit of a chicken-and-egg situation.

And I say to you – the You who feels that you have to stay in contact – can you possibly relax just now, and know that you do not have to make any decision about going No-Contact until you have completed this book?

All you are doing at this stage is gathering information.

This resource will absolutely *not* compel you to go No-Contact.

So there is no danger in allowing yourself to continue reading this book. By the time you come to make a decision, you will have a lot more information. Now, as you access this information going forward, by all means be as cynical and sceptical as you want. You don't believe any of what I say just because I say it: it's my responsibility to make a good case, not yours to automatically believe me. Your responsibility, if you choose to accept it, is just to finish this book and gather the information.

Exercise 1: Write a short contract for yourself to commit to finishing this book so that you can make a full and informed decision about going No-Contact.[1]

1.5: Her *Greatest Hits*

One of the biggest tricks our mind plays with us with regard to our relationship with our narcissistic mother is to make us minimise the toxicity. 'Ahhh it wasn't that bad', we say to ourselves.

This habit of course makes perfect sense because our narcissistic mother taught us all our lives to minimise her behaviour and to invalidate our own feelings about it. However, as understandable as it may be, this trait definitely does not serve us, and we need to change it. And so:

Exercise 2: I offer you now to start writing down[1] what I am ironically calling *Your Mother's Greatest Hits*. By this I mean, of course, all the nasty horrible things she has done, all the times she was mean, all

[1]   You can do this in a notebook, or use the Printable available via the Resources page on donm.info/htgnc-resources, and this applies to all the exercises going forward.

the missed kindnesses: everything. In other words: all the reasons why you might go No-Contact.

Include everything from the biggest to the smallest incident. And as you progress through this resource, add to this *Greatest Hits* list whenever a memory comes to you.

You can use sins of omission too as well as sins of commission, in other words, the things she didn't do that she should have.

You don't want to get upset about these incidents, so don't go into any detail; instead, just write a couple of words which will remind you of the incident. The title of the specific Greatest Hit so to speak.

And then, going forward, if you find yourself thinking something like, 'Ahhh she wasn't that bad,' you have the *Greatest Hits* list which will be proof that yes, she absolutely *is* that bad. Later in the book we'll be sharing other ways to resolve that *she–isn't–that–bad* thought.

You might well find that you don't have to actually read the *Greatest Hits* List, that just remembering its existence is enough to remind you why you're contemplating going No-Contact.

I'll give you a few examples from my own experience:

- Miscarriage
- Wedding
- Handbag/10th birthday
- Car stolen
- Laura/My infertility

- 'Only words'
- Rathmines play.

Now, I know these words themselves won't mean anything to you, and that's okay. Our *Greatest Hits* lists are private to us and don't have to make any sense to anyone but us; I'm only sharing them here as an example of how brief keywords can remind you of the incident without going into any detail or revisiting the experience.

The *Rathmines play* incident was very small indeed: I was acting in my first amateur dramatics play and I was extremely excited and proud. My parents came to see it. Afterwards my mother barely commented on my performance, but went on and on about one particular member of the cast and how good they were. And in truth, that other person was a much better actor than I am. But that person wasn't her daughter, and I felt very let down at her shrugging dismissal of my own performance. I know I wasn't amazing, but mothers are supposed to be enthusiastic regardless, right?

In the grand scheme of things, this is a very, very minor experience indeed, and that is precisely why I tell you about it and encourage you to include such small incidents yourself: because the narcissistic mother ruins everything, both big things and small. And by the nature of life, there are many more small things than big, and those being ruined all adds up to form the map of our lives. Death by a thousand cuts.

And of course, do record bigger incidents too, the way I have recorded miscarriage, wedding and infertility.

Chapter 2
THE GIFTS OF
NO-CONTACT

I would be very remiss if I didn't talk to you about the joys of going No-Contact. Right now it might seem to you that this is all trouble and all problems and all doubts and all fears, and those are all very justified, and we will definitely be going through all of those and helping you over them.

However, I want you to know that the other side of all of those is a life such as you have literally never known before.

As you go through the rest of this resource, this is a way to keep your eye on the prize, so to speak, to know why you are doing this at all.

I don't think you can possibly realise, until you're free of the toxic dynamic, the sheer energy it takes to cope with your narcissistic mother, and how that depletes the energy you should be spending on all else in your life. You don't realise it (yet!) because it is all you have known all your life.

It's like air pressure. Each of us has tons of air pressure pressing down on us all the time, and we're not aware of it because we have known nothing else ever.

And you have not yet ever experienced life without the weight of your mother's narcissism pressing down on you.

However, speaking as someone who *has* experienced that narcissism-free life, it is *everything*.

Now, there *is* a time of transition between now on the one hand and your narcissism-free life on the other, going through the whole process, and we will for sure talk about that, as I don't want to minimise it.

However, once you no longer have to please her and pander to her and worry about what she says and her nasty comments, and organise celebrations without worrying how she will spoil them: everything! Once you are No-Contact, you can live your life without worrying about her reactions and the drama and trauma she would inevitably cause.

You can, quite simply, just go and live your life. How revolutionary is that! You'll have more energy for your own children if you have them, for your own partner if you have one, for your own career, and – above all – for your own life. For *you*!

We will talk towards the end of this resource about how to be in the world as a No-Contact woman, so we won't go too much into it now, but just to let you know that that's what's waiting for you.

I'm going to share stories from other DONMs about their own No-Contact experience, but first let me share my own experience with you.

I won't say it was easy. The freedom from being in contact with my dysfunctional parents gave me space to look at a marriage that had never worked, and I ended up divorced. I do want to stress that my ex is in no way narcissistic or abusive; he is a decent kind man, but our relationship had never worked. Also, because of that divorce there were huge financial worries. It was a very low time. It was not one bit easy. However, in the fourteen years since then, every year has been better than the one before. I am now living the life I should always have been living. I am more confident; I am happier; I have more energy; I have more strength. Now I'm not saying everything is perfect. I am still dealing with the fallout of it all. I am still a DONM, and I would never be claiming that I am sitting at the top of a mountain beatifically meditating, completely enlightened and telling the rest of you to catch up! Nope, my life is still messy and chaotic and stressful: I don't have a perfect life by any stretch of the imagination!

But it is *zillions* of times better than it was when I was in

24

touch with my mother and father and they were sucking every last bit of energy and vitality out of me.

So that was my experience. I'll share now what other DONMs have had to say. These stories are slightly edited for length without amending their meaning. Some DONMs used their names, and others preferred not to, and of course I honour that. Also, of course, all these stories are shared with full permission.

Peggy says she's now happy and peaceful, enjoying a drama-less life. She has time available to establish healthy friendships, and to participate in activities with her husband and children and grandchildren. Her joy increases on a daily basis. She has discovered a new life and the courage to try new activities without fear. She is happier and therefore her family is happier.

Susan says: 'I used to fear going No-Contact. Now it has been three years and I am no longer being abused constantly. I took back my personal power as a human being, and I feel better for it. My only regret is not doing it thirty years ago.'

Lovisa says, 'I have a lot more energy, and I have the peace of mind to take it easy. I don't have to perform in life any more. I feel so much better that I have finally started to bloom because no-one is holding me down.'

Another DONM wrote, 'I'm off to play pickleball and then band rehearsal. I never had time for this before!'

And another DONM says, 'I have been No-Contact for two weeks or better, and I am starting to feel so alive! Maybe it's natural but I catch myself missing her just a little and I want to share my new experiences [with her]. Isn't that strange? But that only lasts a minute and goes away, and it's not as depressing or consuming. You literally feel free. I'm sure this isn't forever. She is my mother and I'm sure I'll eventually have a moment of weakness. But that's okay. This feels too good and things are starting to not be so heavy. I think it might just be okay after all. Wow!'

Another DONM wrote, 'For me, going No-Contact, whilst difficult and sad at times, has given me freedom from all the drama that had become normal. Life is so much calmer and happier now. Who knew? I just thought that's how families were. At first, I didn't even realise No-Contact was possible, but from the moment I decided enough was enough, and I didn't want to deal with the disgusting way they behaved, or for my children to think how they behaved was normal, it has been a tough but liberating experience. [...] Love is about caring, respecting and supporting, and when people don't treat you with these, whoever they are, know that you are worth more, and you don't have to put up with behaviour that makes you sad, angry and hurt. [After No-Contact] watch your life – you! – bloom into who you should be. It does take time but with patience [...] things do improve. My life is still difficult at certain times, but is so much richer now that I have time for other things rather than dealing with their dramas or trying to please those who can never be pleased. [...] So, no matter who judges, I am secure in the knowledge it was the right decision for me, and three years on I still feel the same.'

Another DONM writes, 'It's shocking how much energy I have now to do things that improve my life. My life has completely changed.'

Carrie wrote, 'It's unbelievable how much time I have now to build a healthy new life. I have new things to talk about now besides 'You won't believe what Mom did now' stories LOL. I lost 40 pounds and am recovering from a food addiction. I exercise daily and I joined a few community organisations. My friends say that I glow, and it is obvious that I am happy. My husband said that he is happy to see that I am no longer in so much pain. Life is actually worth living. I am sharing this info in the hope that it might help another person escape this madness. of course people have to make their own decision regarding No-Contact, but I found for myself that I could not start my healing and recovery until I stopped the pain. […] Recovery and healing is finally possible now.

Another DONM wrote: 'Going No-Contact is what finally helped me let go of it all: the guilt, the anxiety, the awful hold she had over me. It is truly empowering to go No-Contact and I would highly recommend it to anyone trapped in the healing process.'

Teressa writes, 'It is a year now and it is the best thing I could ever have done for me. No-Contact has saved me. I do not fret, worry and stress myself as to what is wrong with me anymore. […] I haven't had the battles and controversy for one whole year. It has been a peaceful year for me. I am at peace for the first time I can ever remember. For the first time in my life I am okay with me.'

As Victoria found, going No-Contact can be a complex journey. She writes, 'It has been one year No-Contact. Most of that time was spent grieving, learning and analysing, and now I am on to recovery because my energy is coming back, and my mind is clearer.'

Ali writes, 'Both me and my sister have reflected that in the past year and a half of No-Contact, we have observed ourselves becoming kinder, more compassionate, less prickly, and less reactive in the world and in our interactions with others. The benefits continue to unfold in unexpected and unusual ways.'

Dorrie writes, 'Since I went No-Contact I have been able to quit drinking and have received a Master's degree in Guidance and Counselling, and a Doctoral degree in Education Leadership.'

Another DONM wrote, 'It's been two years. It's been

wonderful, it's been truly wonderful. It takes a while to realise how freeing it is but it really is wonderful.'

Another DONM also has complex emotions. She says, 'I feel incredibly guilty, lonely, angry, sad. I also feel more peaceful, confident and secure. I am no longer an extension, but I belong to myself.'

Another DONM writes, 'I have not had communication with [my Narcissistic Mother] for five years now, and although it was a hard decision to make, it has allowed me to channel my energy into recovering, and finding, and cherishing the light within me.'

Sally wrote, 'Thank you for letting me know I could go No-Contact. It's been my saving grace.'

Another DONM wrote, 'I am happy and at peace since going No-Contact. Mostly I have found myself as I feel there is space to breathe and a weight has been lifted off my shoulders. I can explore things that matter to me without her judgement and negative energy, and focussing on new healthy interests helps me heal. Overall there is less drama in my life which makes it more peaceful. As time goes on I feel less wistful about the mother I needed but didn't have.'

Another DONM writes, 'It has been such a tough three years but yet I am a happier, freer and bigger person as a result of three years of No-Contact. That says it all for me!'

Another DONM says, 'I have been No-Contact with my birth mother now for nearly five years, and it's been by far the hardest but yet the most empowering decision I have ever made.'

Another DONM wrote, 'Sure, there have been moments of pain, deep grief and sadness along the way, and to be honest those moments still arise from time to time, but I know in my bones that I have made the right decision, and I will say that it gets slightly easier every day. The woman I am today in comparison to the woman I was [before No-Contact] is unrecognisable. I have joy, and autonomy over my life, and energy now.'

So, I hope that those quotes have inspired you.

Exercise 3: Start your own *Gifts Of No-Contact* list. At this stage you'll have to use your imagination, but that is perfectly fine. Your imagination will help you realise the possible future you can create. You can use the list above as inspiration, and/or think of all the horrible things she does and put down the opposite of those. For example: *I'll never have to listen to her boring self-indulgent stories.*

Chapter 3
LAST ATTEMPTS BEFORE GOING NO-CONTACT

We're going to talk now about how you might think you need to try once more to fix things with your Narcissistic Mother before making any decision about going No-Contact, that it wouldn't be fair for you to take such an enormous step without giving her every last chance first.

Of course you do *not* need to do this. You can acknowledge that you have tried and tried and *tried* for your whole life, and nothing improved despite all your efforts, and that you have done enough already.

Later we will be sharing a resource (EFT / Tapping) to let you release this feeling that you need to give her one last chance, so with all the information we discuss here, don't feel you have to make any decision on it just yet. You can give her this one last chance later, or not at all, and you'll have a lot more information by the end of this resource with which to make that decision.

So we're discussing this only hypothetically for now, to give you the information.

The first thing is to decide what a good relationship with her would look like. What specifically are you asking for?

Exercise 4: Write down what a healthy relationship with your mother would look like. What she would have to change in order for you to be happy, comfortable, and valued in the relationship. Try to be as specific as you can.

And then, either with or without a list, as you choose, you could sit down with your Narcissistic Mother and say something along the lines of:

'Mom, we need to have a serious conversation. I am not happy with the way our relationship is working, and I would like to discuss this with you to see if we can improve things. Would you be willing to do that?'

In this way, you are opening the door to the concept of a discussion before telling her anything that is wrong with her (which of course is very hard for a narcissist to hear).

Her reaction here will give you valuable information.

She might respond with gaslighting and fury and attack. Something like:

'What are you going on about? Our relationship is working fine. Or would be, if you weren't always looking for things to be miserable about. Honestly I have to walk on eggshells around you as you're looking for insult in everything I say. Nothing I do pleases you! And now you want me to sit and listen to you moan about your made-up complaints. I've better things to be doing with my time!'

This, I strongly suspect, is the most likely outcome.

Or she might do as my own father would every time I tried to sort things out:

'Well you think *you're* so perfect! You're far from perfect, and we put up with all your horrible traits, and you want to talk about *our* foibles! Ha that's a bit rich!'

And that would shut me up, as of course it was designed to do.

Now, with more knowledge and awareness of this all, I wish I had been able to say: 'By all means let's discuss my short-comings. If I'm doing anything to upset you, of course I want to know about it so I can change it. But let's discuss my issues first.'

This still wouldn't have worked, of course, but it would have failed a higher level.

Or, rather than fury, my mother might have burst into tears and wailed, 'You've upset me now!' And that would end the conversation, as it was designed to do.

So it's very likely that your mother won't even *begin* to have the conversation you suggest, but rather she will shut down the conversation.

And if that happens, that is very good information for you. That tells you all you need to know about how willing your mother is to work with you on this. And you could let yourself know that that was her last chance, and she blew it.

But for argument's sake, say she does listen to you. That could theoretically be because she is not a narcissist and you misjudged her all along.

What then?

First, I don't think for one minute this is the case. Think of all the steps you took in order to find yourself reading these words: the searching, the finding, the reading, the investment of time and money. You didn't do that on a whim or because your mother is mildly annoying.

But, if she's not a narcissist, she will respond well and calmly and openly, and you can progress from there.

But it could also happen that your mother doesn't want to lose you, for her own narcissistic reasons: narcissistic supply, drama and so on. And so she might say something like, 'Okay, tell me in what ways you think our relationship isn't working.'

So what do you say to her? If you have your list created, you could share those items with her. Or you could go for top-level changes, for example, you could say to her, 'Just be nicer to me', but the obvious response to that is, 'But I am already nice to you.' Or if you say for her to treat you with respect, she'll insist that she already does that.

What then?

I think the problem is not with any specific actions per se, but with their attitude which leads to their actions. The narcissistic attitude of, *I'm already perfect and your needs are completely irrelevant.* That attitude.

I didn't have this conversation with my parents myself because my own No-Contact journey was quite messy as I didn't have all this information then. However, I have thought of it often in the years since, wondering if there was anything at all I could have done differently to make it work, and I genuinely cannot find anything. What could I have said to them? *'Be nicer to me.'* What does that look like? Nice people don't need directions and narcissists won't understand them. Or, *'Be interested in me.'* But I realised that nobody can force interest, and if they weren't interested in my life, then they just weren't. And perhaps they could have faked it but you know, that wouldn't have worked either. I don't want someone pretending to be interested in me. And if they're not interested, I'm not going to inflict myself on them.

Maybe though, for the sake of keeping in contact, we could focus on our mother's actions and try to control those. 'Please stop criticising what I wear. Please stop dissing my partner. Please stop talking over my child.'[2]

And they might agree to those. But given that there is no substance behind their agreement, no understanding of why it's important, they'll do it the bare minimum they can get away with, and you'll have to constantly police it. What if she says she thought your child was finished talking when he wasn't?

And what if something else comes up that you hadn't thought of: she sneers at your friend's accent maybe. So you

[2] If you decide to go this route, I invite you to check out my book *Become A Boundaries Badass* at donm.info/babb

tell her to stop doing that too. But then you're leaving yourself open to accusations of moving goalposts.

You weren't really. It's still the original goalpost of *Be Nice*. But given that you have to break it down into specific actions, she can spin it as moving goalposts.

However, if she wants you around for her own reasons, she might well agree to all of this, and she'll be nice and kind and interested (or seem to be those things) for a period of time. And there can be huge relief for you in this, huge joy, as you finally have the mother you always wanted.

But if she is a narcissist, this niceness will not – cannot – last, and she'll go back to her normal nasty self.

This is because, for a narcissist, being nice/kind/ respectful goes completely against her nature and it is exhausting for her to do that. Have you ever tried to force magnets together the wrong way, North-to-North say? And how it only works as long as you exert constant pressure, and the minute you relax, the magnets whirl around to their correct orientation?

It's like that for narcissists. So she won't be able to keep being nice and will soon revert back to her normal nasty self.

Or perhaps she will be even nastier, as a) she has all the pent-up nastiness to express and b) she wants to punish you for forcing her to be nice to you.

This will of course be massively painful. To go from (what you thought was) a nice relationship to this vitriol and abuse.

However, even through the pain, this will be essential information for you.

What about trying therapy with her?
As part of trying to work things out with your mother before taking the nuclear option of No-Contact you might say to her:

'Mom, this is serious. I am not happy with the way our

relationship is going. Let's try therapy together to work things out between us.'

She might reject this offer of therapy out of hand. Therapy, after all, means to fix what's broken, and there's nothing broken about her, thank you very much.

And if she does reject it, well, that's good information for you too and we will come back to that later.

However, she might well agree to go to therapy. But! If she does agree, it's only because – in her opinion – the broken thing that needs to be fixed is you.

You would be going to therapy to try to find new ways to relate together in a way that works for you both. She would be going in order to get the therapist to fix you so you remain her biddable daughter. These are very different aims, and so the therapy is doomed from the start for that reason alone.

However, therapy with a narcissistic mother never ends well even without the issue of differing aims. This is because, most often, the narcissistic mother picked the therapist, or it was one she was going to already. This meant that the therapist was already on the Narcissistic Mother's side; especially so if it was her current therapist as that therapist had already heard whole sagas about what a bad daughter you are, how much trouble you cause her, how nothing ever pleases you, etc.

So, in this scenario the mother and therapist would gang up on the daughter, and make her doubly convinced she was the problem, and a terrible person, etc.

I'm not saying that in this case the therapist would be deliberately ganging up on the daughter. (Although she might be; therapists can be narcissists too.) But therapists are only human, and they can be fooled by clever narcissists, and that's why it'd be happening.

I'll go as far as to say that if this is an on-going regular therapist of your mother's, then it's guaranteed, for reasons I explain below, that that therapist will have swallowed the Kool Aid and will believe your mother's lies and that she (your mother) is the poor innocent victim.

No matter how innocent the intentions of the therapist, though, the result would be the same: you being abused further.

The other possibility is that you go to your therapist, who is forewarned about your mother's Narcissistic Personality Disorder (and I do sincerely hope that if you do have a therapist, she fully supports you and understands about Narcissistic Personality Disorder).

Or it might be a therapist new to you both who is knowledgeable enough to identify your mother's narcissism, or at the very least to call her on her behaviour.

What will happen then, guaranteed, is that your mother will find some way to stop going. She'll declare the therapist a quack who doesn't know what s/he's talking about, or declare that her going to therapy is a waste of time when it's YOU who's the problem, or suddenly come down with some illness that stops her going, or financial woes likewise (although those illnesses and financial woes won't stop her doing other things).

And that is why, if your mother has an on-going therapist, that therapist is guaranteed to have been fooled by her, because the very fact that your mother is still going means that she's hearing only what she wants to hear from the therapist.

And all this is why therapy with your narcissistic mother isn't going to work.

Having said all that, there can be reasons why you might agree to going to therapy together, for example, so you can be certain you have done absolutely everything possible to salvage the relationship and can therefore walk away with a clear conscience.

If you do decide to do this, here are a few suggestions:

Make sure you pick the therapist, not letting your mother do it. Even better if it's your therapist to start with (although you may then be sure your mother will accuse that therapist of being on your side and ganging up on her, when the therapist calls her on any of her behaviour).

When you speak to the therapist beforehand, ask him / her what they know about Narcissistic Personality Disorder, and get them to tell you what they know, rather than you asking direct questions. Only pick a therapist who does know about it, and has accurate information that they can give you. You'd be surprised and shocked at how many therapists do not know. And if they baulk at proving themselves to you, then they're not the therapist for you anyway.

You can say, 'I'm interested in coming to work with you with my mother. We're having issues that I believe involve Narcissistic Personality Disorder. Do you know much about that?'

And if they say, 'Yes, yes I do,' you can ask, 'Could you share with me some of your understandings about it?' and then let them speak.

And so, if you find a good therapist who does know about Narcissistic Personality Disorder, you and your mother can go there. The outcome will of course be that the first time the therapist applies the slightest criticism of your mother, that she will throw some kind of hissy fit and storm out and refuse to go back – but you will have got the result of knowing you tried all that you could.

What about giving your mother an ultimatum?
What if you tell her that the situation is so serious, and so down to the wire, that if it doesn't get resolved, you will be forced to go No-Contact. This will let her know how high the stakes are. And, you could argue, asking her to discuss your

relationship and/or go to therapy without telling her what is at stake, is unfair to her.

There is of course no definitive right-or-wrong answer about this, but here are some thoughts:

An ultimatum only shows her how the situation will impact on her. By discussing your relationship at all and telling her it's serious, you are already sharing how badly the current situation impacts on *you*. If its impact on you isn't enough for her, that tells you all you need to know. And so I don't think it's unfair to try to get her to work things out without telling her No-Contact will be a consequence.

Definitely don't give her the No-Contact ultimatum until and unless you are ready to follow through on it. You will know more at the end of this resource and can do it then if you choose.

You can have the discussion/therapy offer without the ultimatum first, and if it doesn't work, go back to her with the ultimatum once you know in your own mind that you are willing to go No-Contact. You can say something like: 'Mom, remember I asked you to discuss our relationship (and/or go to therapy) and it didn't work out for us? Well I need to discuss it with you again because I can't go on like this. If we don't resolve things, I will need to cut off contact with you entirely.'

There are a variety of ways she could respond to an ultimatum. I suspect that the most likely response will be absolute fury and attack. And, of course, if she does that, that is its own information for you.

I said above there is no right or wrong about what you do, but it might be more accurate to say there is no wrong. All paths lead to her revealing herself as a narcissist and you having full information about how unfixable this relationship is, and that is valuable information.

Or she may prove herself to be a non-narcissist. I suspect if you have been brought to the point of reading this, then she definitely is a narcissist. But if you are wrong about her, and she is willing to look at her faults and genuinely change, this approach will facilitate that and you can go ahead and create a loving and mutually respectful relationship with her.

Does all this sound very stressful?

Is your stomach clenching and your heart racing at the thoughts of having a frank and tough conversation with your mother? I know I felt this whenever I tried to resolve anything with my parents. I went into the discussion knowing it would blow up in my face and be a horrendous experience.

If this is happening for you too, then this is also very good information. It is proof that the relationship is dysfunctional. People in healthy relationships discuss and resolve things all the time, and even if that is difficult at times, it is never terrifying.

And if you feel ill and terrified about even the prospect of this discussion, know that you do not have to do this! You do not owe her any last chances.

Chapter 4
THE REALITY
OF NO-CONTACT

No-Contact means that you cut off *all* contact with your narcissistic mother (or any other toxic person).

You do not speak to them, or read, listen or react to any of their communication, ever again. It's that simple, and that profound.

They become just someone that you used to know.

They are a stranger to you.

You do not wish them ill, nor do them harm, just as you do not ill-wish or harm any others of the eight billion strangers you share this world with.

But you do not engage with them, or consider their wants, or let them influence your decisions in any way.

Of course, while it is simple, it is not easy, because you do not share family members with most of those other eight billion strangers, and you do with this one. We will discuss and resolve that and other left-over issues later.

In a way, No-Contact frees both you and your narcissistic mother

It frees you from the endless hamster-wheel of trying to win her affection, her approval, her love. It frees you from endless banging on a door that will never open. It frees you from the exhaustion of pandering to her at the cost of your own quality of life, and that of your own family if you have one. It frees you from constantly being demeaned and undermined and gaslighted and insulted.

And No-Contact is you setting your mother free from the expectation and hope of her ever being a good mother or even a kind person. She will not see it as freedom of course, as we will explore later. But truly it is a gift to her too even though she will never realise it.

There are no good options when it comes to the narcissistic dynamic; there is only your choice of bad options

As the heading says, when you are dealing with a narcissist, there are no good options. They do not leave good options on the table. They force you to pick from a selection of bad options, and we discuss some of those in more detail in this section.

The first set of bad options, however, is the way you are forced into either putting up with an abusive situation, or taking the nuclear option of No-Contact with all the fallout of that. (We'll be exploring the various flavours of fallout later.)

If you stay in contact with a narcissist it absolutely is going to be the same old abusive situation, because the narcissistic mother will not change or treat you better. Narcissists invented *My Way Or The Highway.*

She has created the current dynamic to suit her and her narcissistic needs, so there is zero incentive for her to change it. If it ain't broke, she thinks, why fix it?

And the same applies to her opinion of herself: 'If I ain't broke – and I sure as hell am not – why change?'

The only way you might get her to change a teeny tiny bit, with her always pushing against it, is to use very clear boundaries with her.[3] But this is exhausting, and she will resent it and push against it, and perhaps punish you in other ways for it. So although you can change the relationship in a

[3] And if you think you might go with this option, do check out my book *Become A Boundaries Badass* at donm.info/babb.
But do read the rest of this book first, as you promised yourself you would.

limited and specific way, it'll still be dysfunctional and toxic.

So, stay and put up, or leave. That's it.

Neither of those are good options, and I take no joy in being so blunt about it. This is just the reality of it. But there is some small, good news: at least you get to choose your bad option. And to make a decision about that, you have to look at your other bad options, and we discuss those next.

As we go through this resource, we'll be framing a lot of what we say through the 'bad options' lens, both to acknowledge the reality of what's on offer but also to make sure you realise that you do get to make choices going forward instead of feeling stuck and helpless. There is power in that.

Sadness for sure. But power too.

Let's talk about what exactly No-Contact involves. It might feel strange that I waited this long to define the very topic of our discussion, but I did that for a reason. The fact is that the reality of No-Contact can be quite intimidating and overwhelming, and I wanted you first to hear about the gifts and freedom No-Contact brings, and also to start writing your *Greatest Hits* list.

Now, be very clear as you read this that I am sharing the *what* of going No-Contact here. But do not fret, we will definitely also discuss the *how*. You don't have to worry about that at this point.

That said, here is the reality of No-Contact:

No-Contact means that you never ever have any contact with your narcissistic mother ever again

Now, you can break No-Contact by making a different decision later, and we discuss this in more detail shortly.

But for now, know that No-Contact is The End. No more. Ever. No matter what.

This is the depth and the breadth of No-Contact. If you

go No-Contact your narcissistic mother is dead to you. She is just somebody that you used to know.

You don't send her invitations to any of your occasions, nor accept (or even read) any of her invitations to you

No-Contact is a new paradigm, a new way of living, and as part of that you do not send her invitations to any of your parties or celebrations no matter how important. This will mean she does not attend your wedding or your baby's christening or other huge events.

Remember how she ruined all previous events she was ever at? And how, the bigger the event the more she ruined it?

Those days are over.

Likewise she might send you invitations to some of her events, and you do not attend those either, no matter how big the occasion such as her round-number birthdays.

You do not even answer the invitations.

In fact, ideally you do not even read them, and we'll discuss this more later too.

This is a situation where you might feel rude. But remember: she broke the social contract first.

You do not open or acknowledge any cards or 'gifts' she might send, nor send her any

We'll be discussing later all the various ways your mother might try to pull you back after you go No-Contact, and what to do about them.

For now though, just know that one of those ways might be to send you cards or 'gifts' for your special occasions, or even just for no reason. And if you're No-Contact you will not open them, and certainly not acknowledge them. We will discuss this in more detail later.

You probably do not discuss her with others

We will speak in detail later of the people who come to you to argue your mother's case for her, to beg you to reconsider and so on. There is a lot to say about that.

But for now, just know that you do not have to be part of any conversation you do not want to be part of. You can politely and firmly say, 'I am not going to discuss Mom with you.' You can set boundaries around that: 'If you insist on trying to discuss Mom, then I'll have to leave / hang up.' And then, if they do continue, you enact the consequence and you leave or hang up or whatever is appropriate.

And no doubt they will see that as you being rude, but it's only setting boundaries.

If it is practical, ask others not to discuss you with your mother

You can't police this, of course, but you can certainly ask. And if you think they might not honour this, then just put them on an information diet and don't tell them anything you're not happy for your mother to know.

You don't go to her death bed, nor to her funeral

Yes, this is a huge step and a huge decision, and we will discuss this in detail later in this resource. For now just know that: a) this is part of the huge decision of going No-Contact; and b) you don't have to decide now what you'll do about this topic (as I said, we'll discuss this in detail later and help you decide), just to know that it's part of the whole deal.

5
PRACTICAL REASONS *NOT* TO GO NO-CONTACT

5.1: Introduction

There are some possible circumstances to consider before committing to No-Contact, and which may well limit your options, and we look at those next.

They are:

- If you're living with her
- If she has power over you
- If you're responsible for her care
- Access to other family members
- The reaction of extended family
- Inheritance.

5.2: If you're living with her

You're living with her but are financially independent
If this is the case, then obviously you cannot go No-Contact while you're living with her. The good news is that you have the resources to move out, and I definitely would encourage you to do that anyway, regardless of your No-Contact decision. Living with a Narcissistic Mother brings such stress and doubt and all the bad things that you would be so much better off without them. And then you can consider No-Contact on its own merits.

Exercise 5: Brainstorm ways of moving out.

You're living with her and are financially or physically dependent on her

If you are living with her and dependent on her, then there is no practical way to go No-Contact.

If this is the case, then your absolute job is to do all you can to free yourself from this dependence if at all possible. You cannot have a real choice about going No-Contact (or really, about anything) until you are independent of her.

And of course, the abuse continues as long as the dependence does, and so it's very hard to have the energy to do anything to free yourself. But it's essential. Could you get a live-in job somewhere? Or talk to your local domestic violence centre? The reality is that living with a narcissist depletes you in ways you might not even be aware of because you're so used to it, so it's not surprising if you don't have the energy to start creating a better life for yourself, e.g. enough money to live independently. This is a bit of a Catch-22 situation, and it's why I do urge you to do anything reasonable that you can to move out. Obviously don't go from the frying pan to the fire: use your due diligence and your discernment. But, for example, it might be worth choosing to live somewhere less luxurious than your mother's house.

And even if you're still living with your narcissistic mother, you will still get a lot of value from the rest of this resource: as we said at the beginning, it is really a resource about personal empowerment rather than just about No-Contact, and could provide the seeds needed to break free from your current situation.

> Exercise 6: Brainstorm ways of becoming financially independent of her.

You're living with her and caring for her

If you are living with her and caring for her, the situation is somewhat better, at least in the medium term because the medium term solution is to do all you can, as soon as you can, to move out, or move her out. You can still care for her from a safe distance if needed, as we discuss in the next section.

In the short term, however, you are still stuck with her, unable to go No-Contact. I imagine that she is still abusive even though she is dependent on you – certainly that is the experience of far too many DONMs to write to me who are in this exact circumstance.

If this is the case, you have all the power and she has none. And while it would be completely wrong to use your power to abuse her, it's completely appropriate to use this power to protect yourself from her abuse.

And the way you appropriately use your power is to set, and keep, boundaries, and enforce consequences for breaking those boundaries. (Again I direct you to my book, *Become A Boundaries Badass*: full info at donm.info / babb.)

For example you could say to her, 'If you insult me, I will leave the room and not return for ten minutes,' and then do exactly that. And if she does it again, do the same again.

You cannot appeal to her reason or compassion, but you can train her with consequences. And 'train' might sound like a harsh word, but it is the reality that she has created.

Exercise 7: Brainstorm ways of protecting yourself from her abuse.

5.3: If you're responsible for her care without living with her

We will be exploring shortly how often our beliefs trap us without us realising. And it is possible that you are not as responsible for your mother's care as you think you are. NMs are masters at contrived incompetence to make us responsible for them when they'd be quite capable of looking after themselves.

But for now, we will discuss the topic on the assumption that there genuinely is no other alternative.

In this case, depending on circumstances, you probably cannot go fully No-Contact. But you can possibly make arrangements for her care at one remove. For example, to arrange for her to move into a Nursing Home or Old Folks' Home, and you liaise with the manager there about her care, but without you interacting directly with her.

This is just an example: every situation is different of course. But the principle is the same: see if you can reconfigure things so that you can disentangle yourself from her.

Be aware too, that if your mother is genuinely dependent on you, okay, you cannot go No-Contact, but you have far more power than you realise, because of her dependency. Obviously, as we said just now, I'm not suggesting that you use this power to abuse her back, and I very much doubt you would do that even if I did advocate it! What I do mean though is the power to protect yourself from her abuse, the power to set boundaries and keep to them.

> Exercise 8: Brainstorm ways of caring for her from a safer distance.

5.4: If she has power over you

If your mother has any real power over you, for example, if you work for her, or she owns the home you live in, then do not even try to go No-Contact, both for practical reasons – e.g. you have to communicate about work issues – and also for safety reasons.

Narcissists can be completely vindictive if they are rejected, and it's very possible that she would use her power over you to damage you and punish you by firing you or evicting you. This would leave you in an extremely vulnerable situation.

So I strongly suggest that if this situation applies to you, that you make it a priority to remove yourself from her power, doing whatever it takes, before you consider your next steps.

I know this is easier to say than to do most likely, as changing jobs or moving house are huge steps, and there might be the complication that you are, say, paying under the market rate for rent and can't afford to move to a more expensive home.

The problem is that there is no path to freedom without you removing yourself from her power, because of course she will abuse that power over you if you dare to upset her by going No-Contact.

> Exercise 9: Brainstorm ways of freeing yourself from her power.

5.5: Access to other family members

The sad reality is that your narcissistic mother can, and no doubt will, keep other family members hostage in a way, preventing you from having access to them unless you are in contact with her too.

This most often applies to your other parent, or to younger siblings.

This situation does truly leave you in a no-win situation, and there is no easy answer.

I am assuming in this section that your father (or other parent) is a decent person who you would like to keep in touch with. If he is also a narcissist, or abusive in other ways, then you will most likely not be concerned about keeping in contact with him.

So, assuming you want to stay in touch with him:

In theory you could say it to your father/other parent, 'Look, I'm not going to be seeing Mom any more, but I'd still like a relationship with you. How 'bout it?'

But in practice, that will not work. If he is still with her, he is in a co-dependent relationship with her, by definition. This is because their marriage would never have survived him being independent or willing to stand up to her. Narcissists don't permit that. So if they're still together, it's because he is playing by her rules.

And of course she would not permit him to meet you independently. So, you need to accept that going No-Contact with your narcissistic mother will mean losing contact with your father too, and only you can decide if you are willing to pay that price.

The reality is that it is your father's choice to lose contact with you in this case. It is his decision to choose your mother's whims over a relationship with you.

He could defy her and tell her he will still meet you.

Except, he can't. Not given who he is and the weight of the years of their marriage and their dynamic and their patterns.

You can understand this and even sympathise with him about it. But that doesn't change the reality that he will (most likely) choose your mother over you. And that it is your mother who is forcing that choice.

Another dilemma is if you have adult siblings and aunts/uncles you'd like to keep in touch with.

There are two possibilities here.

What is most likely is that they will be caught in your narcissistic mother's web, and that they will therefore turn on you and reject you if you go No-Contact with her. As is likely to happen with your father, your mother will force them to choose between you and her, and if they're that caught up, they will choose her. And so you have to factor in the reality of losing them too.

Another possibility is that at least one family member is equally stressed in their relationship with her, and your step to freedom will give them the ability to free themselves too, and you and they can bond together.

From my correspondence, this experience is rarer, but it does happen and it's so good when it does.

What you can do is, before you pull the No-Contact

grenade pin, to have a verrrry careful conversation with these people, individually.

You can ask a slightly leading question which criticises your mother the tiniest bit.

So, for example, you could say something like, 'Does it annoy you the way she talks incessantly?'

If the other person bristles, and gets defensive on her behalf, then back off immediately. They are not ready to hear even tiny criticism of her, so they are definitely not ready to hear that you think she is narcissistic.

Hopefully this tiny question is step-backable-from. You can say, 'No, you're right, I understand that she [whatever excuse they came up with],' and then change the subject.

However, it could be that they respond to your question like a drowning person to a life raft. They might say, 'Oh God, *yes*! All the time!'

And then you can take another small step towards an honest conversation, and keep doing that as long as the other person is willing and able to travel with you.

In this case you can help to free them at the same time as you find your own freedom.

Another possibility is that you have much younger siblings, and while you are still in contact you are able to help mitigate some of your mother's abuse of them. If you go No-Contact you will be abandoning them to their fate.

This is a horrendous situation to be in, and as ever with a narcissist, there are no easy answers. Only you can decide what you do.

One factor to consider is that if you go No-Contact, and use the extra energy and time to improve your own life, you can provide resources for them to escape to in time.

Exercise 10: Make a list of who you are likely to lose if you go No-Contact with your mother. Write how willing you are to do this if necessary. Remember that there are no good options, just your choice of bad options.

5.6: Inheritance

The reality is that if you go No-Contact with your narcissistic mother, she will most likely write you out of her will, and you need to factor that into your decision.

There are three things to consider about this.

The first is the size of the expected estate, and your own financial situation. If the estate is small, and you are financially sound, then it will most likely not be an issue at all. But if the estate is large enough and/or your own current circumstances are such that the inheritance will be life-changing, then this is a huge consideration.

Having said that, the second thing to consider is that she might write you out of the will anyway, as a final rejection from beyond the grave. You would have given years and decades of your life in the expectation of inheriting, and not inherit anyway. This is far from a definite, but it is a real possibility.

And the third issue is to factor in the opportunity cost to you of inheriting this money. Be very clear that staying in contact with a narcissist drains you emotionally, physically, psychologically, and spiritually, and this leaves less of everything for you to pour into your own life.

There is no right or wrong to this; just what is right or wrong for you.

Exercise II: Journal your thoughts about possible loss of inheritance, including the price you are willing to pay to inherit. And/or brainstorm how to replicate that lost money yourself.

6
ALL ABOUT
BELIEFS

6.1: Beliefs

If none of the practical reasons to stay in contact apply to you, then it is your beliefs which trap you in this toxic relationship with your mother. And so, in order to navigate and resolve all of this, we need to go into quite a bit of detail about beliefs. This might seem like a digression, but it's not. It is the foundation of everything that follows.

To explain all this, we need to:

- Define what beliefs are,
- show where our beliefs come from,
- explain how those beliefs allow us to navigate the world,
- discuss how some of our beliefs are inaccurate and therefore steer us wrong,
- share information on why we tend to keep thinking the same thoughts,
- and explore how our beliefs talk to us.

And then, later in the book:
- Share how to identify any inaccurate beliefs,
- and then change them for more accurate beliefs so we can live our best lives.

Obviously in the context of this book we will be most concerned about our beliefs regarding our relationship with our mothers, but what you will learn will also be relevant for the rest of your life, and I am so happy and excited to share this with you.

The whole concept of how the brain works, i.e. neuroscience, is hugely complicated and there is a lot that neuroscientists still don't know, and even more that they do know, but I as a lay-person don't properly understand, and so the following explanation of how the brain creates beliefs is beyond simplistic. However, it is sufficient for our needs. I invite you to visit donm.info/htgnc-resources for more details on the whole topic.

What Are Beliefs?

Very simply, our beliefs are the stories we tell ourselves about how the world works.

Biologically our beliefs are held in the brain in what are called *neural pathways*, which are little electrical currents firing between brain cells called neurons. Hence the phrase coined by neuropsychologist Donald Webb: *Neurons that fire together, wire together.*

Where Do Our Beliefs Come From?

We actually *create* our beliefs.

Our brain is desperate to find meaning, and it therefore constantly looks for cause-and-effect. This is why we see – more accurately, create – images in clouds. As psychiatrist Bessel A. Van der Kolk says: 'Because humans are meaning-making creatures, we have a tendency to create some sort of image or story.' And these images and stories become our beliefs.

We create our beliefs this by *gathering evidence based on our observations and experiences*, and then coming to conclusions about it all – in other words, apply meaning to it – and *those conclusions are our beliefs.*

So, say you meet someone new and they tell you their name is Johnny. Or someone else points to him and tells you that man's name is Johnny. It then becomes your belief that his name is Johnny. Easy.

This information – that the man's name is Johnny – creates a new neural pathway between two neurons in your brain as a way to store that information. The new neural pathway is weak and fragile, and just fades away if, for example, you never meet Johnny again and have no need to recall anything about him.

There are two ways, however, in which that neural pathway will be strengthened enough to become entrenched:

- Strong emotion
- Repetition.

If some strong emotion attaches itself to Johnny, such as attraction, or a reminder of someone else called Johnny, or an event at the time such as him causing a fight, or him being in your awareness when something else major happened, then your brain is more likely to create a strong neural pathway and therefore remember him even after just one encounter. This is why we can recall vividly where we were when we heard of some huge news event.

Or, the neural pathway can become stronger and entrenched through repetition, e.g. meeting Johnny a few times and being reminded of his name each time. This is what happens whenever we learn anything by rote such as times-tables or lines for a play.

In our example above you learned Johnny's name directly because he told you. But another way to create a belief is through *deduction*.

Say a stranger joined a group of people you were in, and someone else called him Johnny, you would come to the conclusion (i.e. form the belief) that his name was Johnny. Very logical and appropriate.

You might not even specifically articulate that conclusion to yourself; the information would just slide subliminally into your brain without you ever thinking in as many words, *Oh, his name is Johnny.*

We use our beliefs to navigate the world

As we go through our lives we use our beliefs as maps in a way, to show us what to do in each situation. This is a very efficient system which saves us from having to constantly relearn everything. This is why, for example, you can go into a room you've never been in before, and navigate it well: you will recognise the chairs in the room even though chairs come in a massive variety of shapes, sizes and colours. This might seem like an absurd example, but it only seems absurd because this process is so efficient, so seamless and works so well that normally we don't even have to consider it. If you had to re-learn over and over what a chair was, and how to use one, and multiply that by every aspect of your life, think how difficult life would be to navigate.

But sometimes our beliefs are wrong and therefore steer us wrong

We said before that we create beliefs by assessing the evidence we see and coming to conclusions about it. But, naturally, if we come to the wrong conclusion, then all our beliefs about that topic will be wrong.

This leads to the phrase *Garbage In, Garbage Out.* A process can be perfect, but if the original input is wrong, all subsequent outputs will be wrong too.

So, previously we said that you overheard someone being called Johnny and made the reasonable deduction that that was their name. But Johnny might just be the pet name that other person used for them, or it could be an inside joke that led the other person to call them Johnny.

It was *logical and reasonable* for you to assume his name was Johnny based on the information you had, but in this example you didn't have all the information and hence your belief was *wrong*.

We can see this process very clearly in the hilarious mistakes small children make. For example, my son once told me that French people spell differently than we do: they spell *the* as *ze*. This is because he had read a cartoon where the French person's speech was written to reflect their accent, but he didn't know the concept of spelling phonetically to convey accent, and so, lacking full information, he came to the wrong conclusion.

Here's the essential point: his conclusion was wrong, but based on the evidence he had, it was completely logical and reasonable.

Likewise a friend's small son found his ice-cream too cold, and so he blew on it. He knew that his adults blew on food that was too hot, but he interpreted that as being about food that was the wrong temperature rather than specifically too hot, and therefore also blew on food that was too cold. Same thing: missing information and therefore wrong conclusion, but perfect logic based on the information he had.

These are both trivial and even amusing examples. But because we use our beliefs as maps for living, the same process can cause situations which are neither trivial nor amusing.

Say there was a little girl who had just finished a painting she was hugely proud of, and she hopped off her chair to go and get her parents so she could show it to them. But as she did so, she knocked over her dirty paint water and it spilled all over the painting and ruined it. And then her brain, doing its best to make sense of the world, might conclude there was a cause-and-effect to this and create the belief: *Finishing projects causes them to be ruined.*

She wouldn't even be aware of this new belief, but it would entrench in her brain through strong emotion – i.e. a strong neural pathway would be created – and this belief would then steer her without her even realising, because going forward she would find it difficult, or even impossible, to complete projects.

She wouldn't know why this was happening, and would get frustrated with herself and what she thought was her laziness. But in reality the belief that finishing things causes them to be destroyed was doing its best to protect her from those projects being destroyed. Good intentions; just wrong information.

To complicate things further, we can hold contradictory beliefs. She would also hold the belief that it's essential to finish projects, and those two beliefs would fight with each other. In the metaphor we're using here, these beliefs are represented by committee members, and one committee member would want her to finish projects, and the other would be adamant that she should not.

Or, in our situation, this is why I said at the beginning of this book that you have one committee member who holds the belief that your mother is bad for you and you deserve to be free of her abuse, and at least one committee member who holds the belief that you need to keep in contact with her.

And this is why all this discussion of beliefs and committee members is essential: It explains the dilemma you're experiencing, and we need this understanding before we can go ahead and resolve that dilemma.

And I wanted to describe the biology of beliefs so you can know there's nothing special or sacred about them: essentially they're just bits of wiring.

Why we tend to keep thinking the same thoughts

The brain is a hugely resource-hungry part of our body. The brain represents about 2% of the body weight but it accounts for about 20% of the oxygen and, hence, calories consumed by the body.

Because we evolved at a time when resources were scarce, it makes perfect sense that the brain tries to be as resource-efficient as possible. And to do this, it avoids thinking new thoughts and therefore having to make new neural pathways. As much as it can, it will re-use the already-created thoughts/ neural pathways.

And here's the twist: the more often our brain thinks a thought, the stronger that particular neural pathway becomes because of repetition, and therefore the more that neural pathway fires and the more those neurons wire together, and therefore the more often the brain will automatically think that thought, and therefore the stronger the neural pathway becomes, in an ever-increasing circle. And the more we think it, the truer it feels; but a belief is only true or not on its own merits, not because it feels true. Again: a belief is only bits of wiring.

How our beliefs talk to us

Our beliefs talk to us via automatic thoughts and emotions.

So, anger is telling you that someone is treating you badly, and that would be based on your beliefs about what constitutes bad treatment. I think that we DONMs don't get angry when we should, as we were mis-taught what constituted bad treatment.

Guilt is telling you that you're doing something wrong, and that would be based on your beliefs about what is wrong to do. (And, as you navigate this path of going No-Contact, this one is very important.)

Fear is telling you that something is dangerous to you, and again that would be based on your beliefs about what is dangerous. So for example, someone with a phobia would fear something that, by definition, holds no real danger.

Now, not all emotions are easy to identify and label. They might present just as resistance. This might well be how our painting girl's brain prevents her completing projects.

She wants to complete the projects. She fully intends to. But every time she tries to actually finish it, she gets this resistance, this formless 'ugh' feeling, a sense of dread, maybe exhaustion. Fighting all of that is beyond her, so she decides she'll finish the project later. This decision that she will definitely do it keeps the must-finish-projects committee member happy, and the delay keeps the never-finish-projects committee member happy.

And maybe the deadline for finishing the project approaches, or passes, and this forces her to use sheer willpower to finish it, but that is exhausting. And her self-talk tells her that she's so lazy and disorganised and how she can never do anything right, and she feels awful about herself.

But no. This was nothing to do with laziness or any other supposed character flaw. It was the committee members of her brain doing its best to keep her safe.

We will be sharing shortly how to work better with your beliefs and committee members, but for now just practise becoming aware of your feelings and to observe them rather than 'swimming' in them so to speak.

The English language doesn't help when it has us say *I am sad*, or *I am angry*, and that verb is the same as *I am Danu*, i.e. something that is my identity.

Languages such as Spanish have two words for 'to be': one for permanent traits and one for temporary so we can distinguish these two different situations.

And my own native language Irish says, in direct

translation, Sadness is on me, or Anger is on me. Still not fun in the moment, but it makes it very clear that the emotion is something separate from me, something I am carrying rather than something I am.

To the extent that we are stuck speaking English, let us at least be very clear that our emotions are something separate from us. You could rephrase it as something like, I am feeling anger right now.

Now you might be thinking, hang on, my mother invalidated my feelings all my life. Is this not me doing the same thing to myself?

No, and here's why:

We are doing the exact opposite of invalidating emotions: we are acknowledging them and accepting their presence. We're just choosing not to identify with them.

And so, finally, we get to the point as to why I have taken so much of your time to go into so much detail about beliefs and emotions and neural pathways and so on.

Now that you know that your beliefs can be wrong, no matter how true they feel, and that beliefs are a purely biological process, I invite you to hold your beliefs lightly, to be the boss of them rather than letting them be the boss of you.

This might well seem scary.

Danu, you might be thinking, *my mother gaslighted me all my life so that I didn't know what to believe, and here you are doing the very same thing: making me doubt myself.*

I know that on the surface this might seem the same as your mother's gaslighting, but in fact it is the complete opposite.

Your mother wanted you to *deny reality* in order to believe her version of events.

I want you to *consult with reality* in order to get as near as you can to accuracy.

And in fact, I don't even want you to, as such. It's not my place to want you to do anything. Rather, I *invite* you to do this if you choose. I hope I have made a good enough case that you see the sense of it.

6.2: Society's beliefs and rules

Now, not only do we have individual beliefs, but the culture/society we live in has its beliefs too. By society, I define it in various ways: our whole country/culture, our race, our religion, our community, our family. In this way it is not one society as such, but varied societies.

We, along with most other members of our societies, live by beliefs which we can call rules to live by. And we do this thinking that this is just how things are, rather than it being a societal choice. We think this subconsciously of course: we don't articulate it to ourselves, but I have to use words to explain it.

In other words, these beliefs/rules seem so self-evident that we don't even question them, in the same way that we cannot feel the way air pressure is constantly weighing us down simply because we have never known anything different.

But Society frequently gets things wrong.

It is easier to identify wrong beliefs of other societies, separated from us by either geography or time, rather than the wrong beliefs of our own society and time. Here are some examples of those:

- Women weren't considered competent to vote
- It was okay for children to work very long hours from a young age
- There were public hangings.

Nowadays we see those beliefs and the practices they engendered as abhorrent. But people at the time genuinely thought these things were true and/or okay, and most people didn't even question them. In the same way, we live unquestioningly by our own societal current beliefs. And here is a belief which Society still unquestioningly holds:

All mothers are wonderful and their daughters have to keep in contact with them

And of course, I argue, and hope to provide enough information and perspective that you will agree, that we do *not* have to keep in touch with abusive mothers. That Society is wrong about this.

Society uses peer pressure to keep us in line

There is strong motivation for us to conform to our society's beliefs/rules too, and here is why.

I invite you to look at this diagram called Maslow's Hierarchy Of Needs:

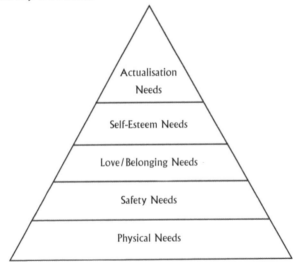

The American psychologist Abraham Maslow posited this hierarchy of human needs. At its base are our physical needs: food, water, clothing, shelter. If we don't have those things, then nothing else matters until and unless we can get those things. We focus only on achieving these things which are necessary for life.

Once we have achieved those necessities, we step up to the next stage, and start being concerned about our safety. That has to come second as we will risk our safety to achieve our basic bodily needs. But our safety is second only to that, and as soon as we can, we start thinking of security, resources and so on.

Once those needs are met, we climb to the next step and start thinking of belonging to our tribe. We evolved with literal tribes, and nowadays we have metaphorical tribes, but the same applies. We want to fit in and belong to our peer group (as soon as it is safe to do so, and we are not competing with them for food, etc.).

And then we move up to more intangible needs such as self-esteem needs and self-actualisation needs.

The bottom two steps – physical needs and safety needs – are about personal survival. I argue, however, that the belonging need is equally about personal survival. Back in the day we had to be in good standing in our tribe in order to survive. Humans – small, weak, slow, no teeth or claws to speak of – needed our tribe literally in order to survive. Safety in numbers; strength in numbers.

This doesn't apply so much nowadays, as society is more complex and there are laws to help us survive even without personal connection. But this is a relatively new phenomenon in our history, and our reaction to shunning or exclusion is still immediate and profound. Think how you feel if someone isn't talking to you, or your group excludes you. This is very deep and very visceral.

So, we have a huge motivation to agree with our society's beliefs and to live by them. But by going No-Contact, we will be going against many of our society's beliefs. No wonder it is so terrifying.

Now, Society clings hard to its rules. So if you do decide you will not be in contact with your abusive mother, that you will not care for her in her old age, etc, then for sure Society will have an opinion on that. It will disapprove of you and tut-tut at you and judge you.

That still doesn't mean Society is right, though. It just means it's loud.

And you can metaphorically cover your ears and *la–la–la* at all the disapproval and tutting, and we will share later in this book ways to help you do that.

Exercise 12: Write a list of all the thoughts that come to you when you consider going No-Contact. You can add to this as new thoughts occur to you. These thoughts are most likely your beliefs about the topic. Or, if they are questions, ponderings and wonderings, such as, 'Why am I not allowed to go No-Contact?' write those down too. You'll get to answer them later.

7
HOW DO YOU KNOW WHAT YOU BELIEVE?

7.1: How do you know what you believe?

If, as we have discussed, we create many of our beliefs without realising, how do we know what our beliefs are? I know Exercise 12 asked you to write down your beliefs, but those are only the ones you're aware of. Many more lurk under the surface, which is why we said you can add to the list later.

Below, we share amazing tools for identifying your beliefs, but first we can say this:

By their fruits you shall know them.
If beliefs steer our actions, when we study our actions we can reverse-engineer to see clues to what beliefs lay behind them.

The painting girl being unable to finish projects is a perfect example of that.

We will explore this in more depth, but for now, know that by observing what you actually did (say, let a deadline go past without applying for a wanted job) rather than what you thought you wanted (to apply for the job) then there are some blocking beliefs there. You might not yet know exactly what they are, but you know they're there.

Another option is to:

Listen to your self-talk
This can be difficult as the thoughts come and go in an instant, so don't fret if you don't catch them all. Any that are caught will help you understand what's going on.

In our job example, as you consider applying, you might find yourself saying/thinking things like:

- They'd never hire me.
- They'd laugh at me.
- I'm useless
- Who am I to apply for that job?

Here are some other ways to identify your beliefs via your self-talk:

Look out for the words:

- 'But'
- 'Because'
- 'Should'
- 'Therefore' (this word is often implied rather than stated)

Every time you say 'but' you are exposing a belief: 'I'd love to go No-Contact, but …'.

Every time you say 'because', there is a belief too: 'I can't go No-Contact because …'.

Anytime the word 'should' appears, yep, another belief: 'I should stay in contact/look after her.'

Watch out for hidden *therefores*: 'I can't go No-Contact because she is old and therefore I am responsible for taking care of her.'

7.2: Freewriting

Freewriting is a superb way of dialoguing with your subconscious to see what's really going on for you, and to discover your hidden beliefs.

How Do You Know What You Believe?

In order to do freewriting, get yourself a pen and notebook, preferably an A4 (or letter-sized in the U.S.) to give you good space to write. (Or, you might like to use the Printables available via donm.info/htgnc-resources.) Also, make sure it's not too fancy a notebook so you don't feel pressure to write to a high standard to live up to the quality of the paper.

And then, at its simplest, you write for a pre-decided amount of time or number of pages. This work is completely private; you will not be showing it to anyone, so fear not.

There are various variations you can choose from:

- You can freewrite with no goal in mind, to see what your subconscious would like to say to you;
- or you can start with a question, e.g. 'What's blocking me from applying for that job?';
- or you can write letter a letter from you to you, i.e. from one aspect to another, e.g., 'Dear Me who doesn't want to apply for the job ...' or, 'Dear You who's insisting on applying for that job ...';
- or you can write dialogue between the different committee members so all aspects get their say. When I'm doing this I use an asterisk: * and a tilde: ~ to distinguish who is 'speaking' at any given time.

Now, here is the most important thing: when you start a freewriting session, *you do not stop writing* until the time is up or number of pages is done. What will happen is that your conscious brain will want to censor, and edit, and decide what to write. And you already know what your conscious mind thinks so that is no use to you.

Instead you want to let your subconscious mind (i.e. your

hidden beliefs) get a look-in for once. And you do that by writing without stopping. If you cannot think what to write, write exactly that: *I don't know what to write.* And write that over and over until another thought comes into your mind (and it will), and you write that down then. Or if you're frustrated and bored with the exercise, write that! *What a stupid exercise, I should be doing something else instead.*

When you are freewriting you are in charge of *quantity* only; you do not have to worry about *quality.* Your job is to show up and write the pre-decided amount; that's it. Whatever calibre of words end up on the page is not your responsibility.

Don't worry about spelling mistakes or punctuation or keeping to the lines or the quality of your handwriting. I find that when I start a freewriting session my writing starts off very neat, but as I progress it gets looser and bigger and wilder, and I start doing the handwriting equivalent of typos: I know the spelling, but write the word wrong anyway, and punctuation gets forgotten as the sentences run on and on and on. And all of that is more than okay.

Try to write in a spirit of discovery, interested to see what comes out without being attached to any specific content.

And prepare to be amazed at what insights you receive about yourself, your beliefs, your perspectives, your life: everything!

And of course, in our specific situation, you can use freewriting to explore your current blocks to going No-Contact: your Blocking Beliefs in other words. Later we'll be sharing a wonderful way of resolving those beliefs, but for now the aim is to discover them.

And you can also use freewriting all the time, for all sorts of reasons in your life.

Exercise 13: I offer you to try freewriting now: Set a timer for 10 minutes, and just write. You can write about whatever you like, but in our context, why not write about your No-Contact feelings/thoughts.

Here are some starting ideas:

I'd like to go No-Contact but ...
I wonder what a No-Contact life would be like ...
I can't imagine life without my mother ...
The idea of No-Contact scares me because ...

Now, don't get too hung up on any of this. This is just to practise the skill. And whatever comes up in your freewriting, we will no doubt be discussing and processing as this resource progresses.

7.3: EFT / Tapping

I share here an absolutely wonderful process called EFT/ Tapping.

Officially it is called Emotional Freedom Technique, and that's where we get the acronym EFT from. And it involves tapping on acupuncture points, so it's often called Tapping for short, hence the name EFT/Tapping.

This process is called Emotional Freedom because that's exactly what it does: gives emotional freedom.

And more, it helps to first of all identify your Blocking Beliefs, and then helps to change them for better/truer ones if needed. It is the perfect tool to use on this journey to your freedom.

EFT/Tapping is a very simple, easy-to-use, painless process. It is easy and robust – you cannot really get it wrong. It puts huge power literally at your fingertips, and I am going to share how to use it for helping you on this Roadmap To Freedom.

> As you go through this, know that you take full responsibility for your experience with it. I believe it to be safe, or I wouldn't be sharing it of course, but I cannot take responsibility for any adverse reactions you might have. Use your discernment here.
>
> Now, neither do I want to scare you off: as I say, I think this is very safe and gentle, but I just need you to be in charge of your own experience.

The first thing to do is to learn how to do EFT/Tapping, and the next section shows you that.

Using EFT/Tapping to discover your hidden beliefs is simplicity itself. Just use the tapping process with the issue you are aware of. Let's pick as an example your resistance to applying for a job.

As you tap, 'This resistance to applying for the job,' on the various points, a new thought will come to you. It might arrive and disappear before you can identify it, and that's okay. Just keep tapping and it will end up staying long enough for you to know what it is, and that is your hidden belief. It will be a statement, an argument in a way, from the committee member who thinks it's not safe to do the thing, in our example, applying for a job. So the thought, the realisation, the awareness, will come to you, say: *They'll all laugh at me if I apply for the job.*

How Do You Know What You Believe?

And, at its simplest, that is how you use Tapping to identify a belief. In practice, there will most likely be many beliefs, and you can use Tapping to identify them all, and to transmute them all into beliefs which serve you. See the information in Chapter 8 for more on how to do this.

The first thing to do is to learn the Tapping Points. Either (preferably) watch the video at this link on my website donm.info/htgnc-resources and/or read the instructions below.

Here's an image representation of the tapping points (see pp. 88 – 89). Note that although the point is only shown on one side of the body, the points are actually duplicated on both sides (except the central ones of 5 and 6) and you can use either, or both.

The first thing to do is to familiarise yourself with those points. Practise tapping on them. The tapping should have a nice resonance, like a drum – a nice beat. It should be hard enough to feel, but definitely not hard enough to hurt. If in doubt, tap more softly. As you tap you might find that certain points are tender; in this case, just tap more gently on those. EFT should never hurt you.

Sometimes you can get upset while you're doing EFT. This is totally normal if you're releasing past upsets. The crying is not caused by the EFT; it's you experiencing what's already there. Like pus coming out of a wound, it's not pretty, but it shows you're on the way to clearing out the old messy stuff. If you do start crying, just keep tapping as you cry. This crying will be very cathartic and releasing and healing, rather than tight and painful. It's hard to describe, *but it's part of the healing and not part of the problem*. It can be intense though – just go with it, accept it rather than fighting it, and above all keep tapping.

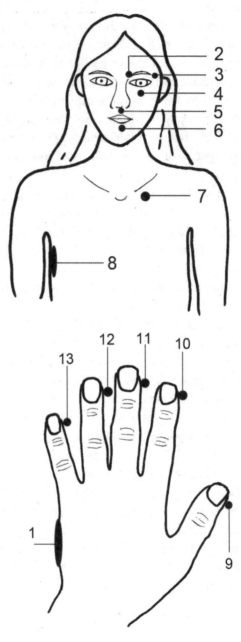

POINT NUMBER	NAME OF POINT
1	Karate Chop (The fleshy bit of the hand you'd use to do a karate chop)
2	Inner Eye
3	Outer Eye
4	Under Eye
5	Nose (Called this even though it's actually under the nose)
6	Chin (Called this even though it's just under the lower lip, before the crease where the chin starts)
7	Collarbone Point. About an inch (2.5 cm) below your collarbone and 2-3 inches (5-8cm) out from the centre of your body.
8	Underarm. This point is hard to illustrate in a graphic – it's actually under your arm, about 4 inches (10 cm) directly below your armpit. For a woman it's where her bra-strap sits and for a man it's on a line with his nipples.
9	Thumb. The point is on the skin alongside the nail for all of the finger points, on the side of the finger nearest the body.
10	Index Finger
11	Middle Finger
12	Ring Finger
13	Little Finger

You shouldn't experience any bad side effects when doing EFT (but as always, you take responsibility for your experiences and do it at your own risk). What you might experience though are some or all of the following:

- Tiredness. If you've done a big session and shifted a lot of stuff, you can be very tired for a while after it. This is perfectly normal. Try, therefore, not to do the tapping before any big occasion for which you need to be fresh.
- Harmless physical reactions such as tummy rumbling, burping or yawning – these are all signs of release, i.e. of the 'stuff' shifting and evaporating. These things don't need to happen for EFT to work, so don't panic if they don't. But don't be surprised if they do happen.
- Occasionally, tearing of the eyes that's not crying – just a kind of release of the tear ducts. This doesn't often happen, but again, don't worry if it does.

Exercise 14: Practise the Tapping process.

Drink a glass of water before you start – the tapping works much better if you are well-hydrated. Get a paper and pen / pencil, or use the scorecard printable available for free at donm.info / htgnc-resources.

Sit as comfortably as you can. Sit upright, but relaxed. Do not cross your ankles.

Define your issue in a short sentence, as best as you can, e.g: 'I'm scared to let anyone see my work.'

Say this out loud and tune into yourself to see how true that is for you, i.e. how well it 'sits' or resonates with you.

Then write down how true this is for you on a scale of

0–10 where 0 is 'No fear at all, let them look!' (obviously you're not there or you wouldn't be tapping for this issue) and 10 is 'I'm completely scared.'

Make sure to write down your score. It's important to write it down rather than just remember it as it gives a tangible indicator of your progress.

And then, start tapping on each point in turn.

On your Karate Chop point (the fleshy side of your hand), say as you tap:

Even though I [have this issue] I accept myself completely and fully. (Obviously, say your actual issue here, and every time the example shows [have this issue].)

Do this three times.

Then tap on each of the other points in turn, saying [have this issue], i.e. whatever your issue is. In our example, 'I'm scared to let anyone see my work'.

And then repeat: Karate Chop x 3 with the full 'Even though ...' statement, and the other points with just your issue.

It's very possible that you will refine your issue as you tap, that you realise, say, that it's only people you know that you don't want to see your work. In that case, amend the statement accordingly.

Every so often, check on your score to see if it has diminished, which it should, and keep going until it's 0 and you have, in our example, full confidence and peace about letting people see your work.

There may be more issues blocking you, so just get rid of those too.

This work can be done in small bursts of course. About 15 minutes a day is loads of time.

You can use the tapping in the moment if anything is distressing for you, e.g. if you get a rejection email, until it passes and you have peace about that. And remember we said that the more comfortable you are with failure, the more inevitable is your success. This process is to help you become comfortable with failure as part of the journey to success.

If the tapping isn't working for you ...

As you're tapping and following the video script, you should find that your score is decreasing. It could happen quickly, or slowly, but it should happen. But sometimes, it just doesn't shift at all.

Here are some causes of why the tapping doesn't work, and the cure. Try these in the order presented.

Dehydration

If you're dehydrated it can stop the Tapping from working. Drink a big glass of water and try again. You may well find that the Tapping starts working really well once you've done that. If not, go onto the next step, below.

Emphasis

When you're following the script, don't just recite the text. Say it with meaning, speak it loudly - even shout it, if you have the privacy to do that. There is something very freeing and powerful about shouting or speaking loudly about your issues, and it adds to the power of tapping. And emphasise the power words. So instead of just saying, 'I do deserve to heal', for example, stress the word 'do': 'I **do** deserve to heal'.

Concentration

If you're not concentrating on the tapping, it doesn't work as well. Try to think about what you're saying rather than just repeating it by rote. And make sure you have no other distractions, so don't do it while you're watching television or playing computer games or any other distraction.

Resistance to getting over the issue

Sometimes you will have resistance to getting over this issue. It could be that it doesn't feel safe to get over it, or you don't feel you deserve to, or other such reasons. If this is happening to you, then you'll understandably block your own healing, even at a subconscious level. If this is the problem, step away from the issue and work on the resistance to healing it. It's as if your goal is to saw wood, but you discover the saw is blunt. The solution is to temporarily leave the wood and go and sharpen the saw. That's what we're doing here.

Tap using statements like: *It's not safe to heal the issue − I have blocks to healing the issue − For some reason I want to hang onto the issue − I'm not ready to let go of the issue − There is some benefit to me to keep the issue.* And then try the EFT again on the issue and see if it's working then.

8
HOW TO MANAGE
YOUR BELIEFS

Now that you know how beliefs are formed, what do you do with that information?

Later in this resource we'll be going through all the beliefs that keep you trapped in the toxic narcissistic dynamic. I hope I will make a good enough case that you see the sense of another perspective, one that frees you.

However, there is a big difference between knowing and KNOWING. By this I mean that you can know something in your head, intellectually, but you do not KNOW it in your heart, in your gut, in the deepest part of you. And it's the KNOWING that directs your actions.

Luckily there is a way to make sure you get to KNOW something that you intellectually know is true. And this is of course EFT / Tapping.

We use EFT / Tapping not just for identifying our beliefs as we did previously, but for changing them if needed. We'll be sharing shortly how to do that.

8.1: Committee Meeting

Remember how we already said that we are run by committee? Well, the exciting news is that we can call a virtual committee meeting and discuss and negotiate with each of our committee members, and in so doing resolve their concerns in a way that works for you *and* them.

Is this real? Is it metaphor? Is it just a way of working with your brain? I've no idea, but I love the results and I am excited to share the process with you.

This concept of committees is a mixture of the following concepts:

- Ideas I was exploring myself as I explored the reasons why I would keep sabotaging myself and why others do so too: it seems to be a universal human problem.
- Inner child work based on writers such as John Bradshaw and Lucia Capacchione – but inner child work expanded as we have inner all ages and inner attitudes and so on.
- Matrix Reimprinting, created by Karl Dawson, which is a way of using Tapping in your imagination directly with the younger You who experienced the trauma you're trying to resolve, rather than the today-you who is experiencing the fallout of that trauma.
- Internal Family Systems (IFS) created by Richard Schwartz. What I have been calling committee members, IFS calls 'parts'.

And I am beyond excited to share all this with you as a resource to help yourself resolve your blocks to going No-Contact, but you can also use it in the rest of your life.

As you go through this, as with the Tapping, know that you take full responsibility for your experience with it. I believe it to be safe, or I wouldn't be sharing it of course, but I cannot take responsibility for any adverse reactions you might have. Use your discernment here.

Now, neither do I want to scare you off: as I say, I think this is very safe and gentle, but I just need you to be in charge of your own experience.

As you prepare to 'meet' your committee members, let me

remind you that there are no bad guys here. All the committee members are *you*, doing their best to keep you safe and happy (in that order: safety trumps happiness, exactly as in Maslow's Hierarchy of Needs). These committee members absolutely have the best of intentions; it just might be that they have wrong information about how to meet your highest good. Or they might have such good points that you come around to their way of thinking. In this way, Committee Meetings are a way of accessing more of your wisdom.

I came to this technique because I was so frustrated with my incessant self-sabotage, but I have come to realise that it's not self-sabotage at all, but protection. It is, in fact, an intervention against what the committee member thinks is a serious danger. And a small pain is worth it to prevent a bigger one, just as, if you grabbed a child to pull them out of the path of an oncoming car, you wouldn't care if you bruised that child's arm in the process.

The whole process of discussing and negotiating with your committee members might sound strange, but don't let that intimidate you: this is *you* talking to *you*, and so it will most likely flow well. Think of it like you going to a friend to discuss something, but that friend is guaranteed to be on your side. There's no incorrect way to do this; you cannot get it wrong, so just relax and enjoy the process rather than feeling there's some standard you have to reach.

I share the process below, and then share a summary below that.

How to hold a Committee Meeting
Sit yourself down
Sit yourself somewhere private and comfortable. Be sure to have a drink of water with you.

As with any meeting, you will need to start with an

Agenda, and finish with the Minutes of what was agreed to during the meeting. So, do have a pen and paper with you (or the printables available via donm.info/htgnc-resources).

You can speak these Committee Meetings or freewrite them. Again there are printables available for freewriting the Committee Meetings, but they're not necessary as you can just use a notebook.

If you speak them, you might like to record the sessions but this is absolutely not essential.

You might find it easier to close your eyes, especially if you are speaking rather than writing. If you like, you can imagine yourself in a special place, either real or imaginary: the beach, woodlands, etc., but this is absolutely not necessary.

If you are speaking rather than writing, I find it best to speak aloud, to help with concentration. If you're just thinking quietly it's far too easy to get distracted. You might find yourself thinking something like, *I'd like to invite x committee member to join me, oh I wonder did Moira ever get her car problems sorted, I must ask her, and that reminds me it's Philip's birthday, must send him a card* ... and so on.

The fact you're speaking aloud is another reason to make sure you have privacy. You don't want to have to censor your discussion in any way.

Write the Meeting Agenda

This will be a one-item Agenda, and is just to clarify your thoughts about: a) which Committee Member you are going to speak with, and b) what you're hoping to achieve. In our example it will be: *Meet with a Committee Member who doesn't want me to go No—Contact, discuss their concerns, and come to a mutual agreement.* You can write this on your own paper or on printables.

Invitation

Literally say aloud, or write: 'I'm now inviting the Committee Member who thinks I shouldn't go No-Contact to come and meet with me so we can discuss their concerns.'

And then wait for them to show up, which they will.

You might experience them as an image of some kind, or feel a sensation in your body.

Thanking them for joining you

Thank this committee member for turning up to meet you.

Try to feel genuine gratitude, both for them turning up, and also for them holding this role all these years, which was always done to protect you despite how it might feel right now. Remember: there are no bad guys in this process.

If you feel in any way negative towards them, for example, angry that they are blocking you from something you want to do, remind yourself that they *are* you: a part of you who definitely has your best interests at heart, but who just has different information. They are (possibly) mistaken, but they are never malicious.

This process cannot continue unless you feel warmth and even gratitude towards them. Remind yourself that you are not on an opposing side to them, but rather are allies who both want to create the best life for you, and who just need to discuss how to do that. Knowing this should help you resolve any negativity, but don't forget you can use Tapping to let go of any negative feelings if needed.

Don't move forward in this process until you feel warmth and gratitude towards them, for obvious reasons: if you feel adversarial, guess how the dialogue will go! Even assuming they will speak to you at all.

Naming them

Ask them what their name is and wait for them to tell you. It might be a real name such as Madge or George, or a descriptive name. In this example let's say our committee member's name is Blocking. Make a mental or written note of that, and indeed you can use their name when speaking to them during the rest of the conversation.

Ask them if they are willing to discuss this issue with you

They might not be, for example if they don't trust you yet. If this is the case, ask them what you can do to help them trust you enough to have the conversation. Remind them that they hold all the power here, in that you cannot force them to do anything. Remind them too that *you are them*, a part of them who wants the best for you and just has different information, that you are not on an opposing side to them, but rather are allies who both want to create the best life for you, and who just need to discuss how to do that.

As you do this process more, you will find that the committee members will trust you more, for reasons I'll share below.

Conversation to resolution

You then begin the conversation with them and it might go something like this:

You: I know that you have good reason for blocking me from going No-Contact, and I wonder would you share with me what that is?

[Try to keep your questions mild and interested, rather than being like an interrogation. You are genuinely trying to find out what the Committee Member's reasons are, rather than trying to catch them out.]

Committee Member: Because it would hurt her too much.

[And can you see how this is a perfectly valid reason?]

You: Yes, it probably would. But maybe we could let that be okay?

CM: No! Of course we can't.

You: Why not, do you think?

CM: We have to be better than her. Just because she's cruel doesn't give us the licence to be cruel back.

[And this is a very valid opinion, isn't it? It makes perfect sense how the Committee Member came to this conclusion.]

You: Absolutely. I fully agree. We want to act in integrity, don't we?

CM: Absolutely. We will not sink to her level.

You: I agree on that too. I wonder, though, could we explore a bit more about whether it is cruel to protect yourself from someone's abuse. I'm considering just to cut off contact, not to proactively do anything bad to her.

CM: Welllll …

[The Committee Member is a bit confused now; their previous certainty wavering a bit. You give them some space to think about it before continuing.]

After a few moments you might continue: If we had our way, nobody would be hurt. Our ideal would be to have a loving and mutually respectful relationship with her, wouldn't we?

CM: Yes. That's true.

You: But she doesn't give us that option, does she?

CM: No. True. We have tried before, I know that, but she wouldn't listen. She just accused us of being horrible to her.

You: Exactly! So the way it is now, either *we* are hurt by the continued relationship, or *she* is hurt by it ending, right?

CM: Yes.

You: And she is the one forcing that choice, right?

CM: Yes.

You: So if we end it, really, she's the one causing her own hurt.

CM pauses to think about it, and again you give them space. And then they say: Yes. Yes, she is.

You: We can regret that she is hurt, but we don't have to sacrifice our well-being to prevent it, I think. What do you think?

CM: I agree.

You: So you don't have to stop us going No-Contact anymore?

CM: No. No I don't.

New job/role for them

You: So now that you no longer have to hold that job of making sure she's not hurt, what would you like to do next? You could take on a new job, or just rest and play as you choose. What do you think?

The Committee Member will choose then what they want, and whatever it is, you give it to them. If they want a whole water-park for themselves to play in, you imagine that, and there it is, in an instant. Often the Committee Member is very tired from holding a tough role all these years and is more than happy to retire and just play.

Or they might choose a job that's the opposite of their old one, e.g. in this example they might want the role of reminding you that you matter too and that you don't have to let people abuse you. They may well choose a new name for themselves too as part of the change. In our example it could be now Alerting.

You might find too that as you go through this process their physical appearance changes. They might go from hunched to standing straight. They may change size. They may look happier. Don't be surprised if this happens, and in fact it's something to be celebrated.

Once you have thanked them for meeting with you and sent them off for their new role, you then check in with yourself to see how you feel about going No-Contact now. Don't be surprised if you still feel resistance to the idea. This is because you might well have other Committee Members who have other good beliefs that make them think you need to stay in Contact, and you need to speak to them too. Later in this book we will go through all possible beliefs and resolve them as needed.

Write the Minutes
Write down the agreement you and the Committee Member came to. It is very possible that as part of the discussion you had to agree to some commitment, for example, to check back in with this Committee Member at a given time to see how they're doing with the new role, and if so, write this down too. And it is essential that if you make a commitment, you keep to it, partly because you said you would, and partly because this teaches the Committee Members that they can trust you.

Don't go into this discussion assuming that you have all the answers; the committee member can contribute wisdom to this too.

This is a genuine discussion and problem-solving session, rather than you imposing solutions. The committee member might propose a good solution or compromise. For example, I was doing this work with one DONM whose committee member was willing to allow her to go No-Contact if she would agree to leave the door open to her mother genuinely changing. This was easy to agree to, and I share later how that would work in practice.

Good questions to ask the committee member

- What are you protecting me from?
- What bad thing will happen if you give up your current behaviour?
- How can I help you feel comfortable enough to reconsider your position?

Using Tapping with the Committee Member
Sometimes the committee member is stuck on an issue and it's just not shifting by discussing it with them. In this case I ask them would they like me to use Tapping on them for the stuck issue, and in my experience they always say yes. In this case I simply imagine myself touching all the tapping points on their body in turn, and those points lighting up with a red light as I do, while we repeat the stuck issue, e.g. 'Not allowed to go No-Contact'.

If they are a non-human shape, which sometimes happens, I just use my best guess as to the tapping points, and it works anyway.

In my experience tapping in this way works even more quickly than it does in the real world, it's amazing to have your committee member make those powerful shifts.

One thing I was working on for myself, the committee member was convinced that if I resolved that issue I would literally die. Given that risk, you can see how they worked so hard and undertook as much self-sabotage (really, interventions) as they needed to make sure I didn't resolve the issue. I used the Tapping on them and it resolved in about two minutes, and they were able to say to me, completely happily, that it was okay now if we resolved the issue, and I went on to do so. I never found out how or why that committee member created that belief, but it didn't matter once I was able to resolve it.

Committee Meeting Summary
1. Find a comfortable and private location.
2. Write down the meeting agenda.
3. Invite the relevant Committee Member to join you and wait for them to arrive.
4. Once they arrive, thank them for coming to meet you.
5. Ask them their name and make a mental or written note of that.
6. Ask them if they're willing to discuss this issue with you, and if not, discuss with them what would help them to be willing.
7. Have a genuine conversation with them until you come up with a solution you're both happy with.
8. Write down the Minutes of the meeting.

8.2: Simple Tapping session

Now that you know the tapping points, it's time to see how Tapping works in practice.

So, at its simplest, what you do is to think of an issue you'd like to resolve (or, in real life, issues often present themselves to you without you having to go looking for them!).

This issue can be something from the past, or something

quite recent. The only condition is that it's something that still upsets you, because obviously if it doesn't upset you, then there's no problem to be resolved.

We'll pick as an example a specific time your mother yelled at you.

Choose a title for the event. Make it something short and easy to say. It doesn't have to make sense to anyone else, once you know what it means. In our example, *My Mother Shouted At Me*, would work perfectly. However, remember we spoke before about your mother's *Greatest Hits*, and I had the example of *Rathmines Play?* Well, *Rathmines Play* would work well as a title too.

Think of that specific occasion where she shouted at you, and ask yourself: On a score from 0–10, where 0 is completely calm, and 10 is totally upset, what is the level of your upset now? Just tune into your body to feel what the score might be. If you don't know, just guess; this will be close enough. This score isn't an exact science, it's just a way of keeping track.

Make sure to write down your score rather than just remembering it, and you can use just a piece of paper for this, or the printable Tapping Scoresheet available as part of this resource at donm.info/htgnc-resources.

There are two reasons to write down your score: the first is that the Tapping works so well that you can end up underestimating how bad you originally felt once the issue begins to resolve itself, and secondly, that it allows you to track your progress. If you don't track, you might start off upset, and after doing Tapping you are still upset, so you think it doesn't work. However, if you know that you started with say a 9 of upset, and you're now at a 6, you'll realise that you definitely are making progress even if the issue isn't fully resolved yet.

Then you slot your issue into the following Tapping Statement:

Even though [the issue] I deeply and completely accept myself.

So, in our example:

Even though my mother shouted at me I deeply and completely accept myself.

Or, in our other example:

Even though Rathmines Play I deeply and completely accept myself.

Now, *Even though Rathmines Play* doesn't make sense grammatically in any way, but it still works for the Tapping. What you are really saying, and indeed could say, is *Even though she was so dismissive of my performance when I did that play in Rathmines* ... but *Even though Rathmines Play* is just shorter to say and works just as well.

If you can bring yourself to complete the Tapping Statement by saying: *I deeply and completely love and accept myself*, then that's even better. You don't have to believe it, but if you can say it without distress, do. But if not, *I deeply and completely accept myself* is fine too.

Then you say the Tapping Statement three times in total while tapping on your Karate Chop Point:

Even though my mother shouted at me I deeply and completely accept myself.

Even though my mother shouted at me I deeply and completely accept myself.

Even though my mother shouted at me I deeply and completely accept myself.

And then you tap on all the remaining points in turn whilst just saying the issue: *My mother shouted at me.*

By tapping on all the points in turn you'll end at your Little Finger point, which brings you back to being beside the Karate Chop.

This is called a Round of Tapping.

You repeat this whole process, i.e. a Round of Tapping, say three or four times; the exact amount is not important. And then you check in with your score again. It should have diminished, and that is how you know it is working. And so you keep doing this, checking in with yourself periodically, until your score is a zero of upset.

Now, in practice it isn't usually this neat, which is why The Tapping Tree is more realistic of how it all works and I invite you to check that out next.

8.3: The Tapping Tree

The Tapping Tree is the name I have given to the process of Tapping where you do deep dives. Let me explain.

As with the Simple Tapping you start by defining your problem as a succinct statement: with your presenting issue, in our example: *I can't bring myself to apply for that job.*

Don't get hung up on the exact wording; once *you* know what you mean by it, they are the right words. There's nothing magic or arcane about Tapping, where you have to use exact words and face east and burn incense or whatever ... This process is very robust.

In truth, the statement doesn't even have to be succinct; it can be as long and convoluted as you like. It's just easier to say succinct statements which is why I recommend that.

Then, write down your score on a 0–10 scale.

And then you start tapping using the process already explained, with your statement as your tapping statement. In our example: *Even though I can't bring myself to apply for the job, I deeply and completely accept myself* x 3 for the Karate Chop and then *I can't bring myself to apply for the job* as your statement for all the other points in turn, and repeat.

What will happen as you tap is either that resistance will vanish (not likely), or more likely that a new thought will come. This is a foundation thought: a reason why you can't bring yourself to apply for the job. The committee member who's trying to keep you safe will present its argument, e.g. *They'll only laugh at me.*

Write down your 0–10 score on that, and use that as your new tapping statement. So you leave *resistance to applying for the job* for the moment, although you will come back to it.

Tap for the statement *They'll only laugh at me* until that is a 0 or another statement comes up. It could be a memory, e.g. *They laughed at me in school that time I spilled the paint.*

You may not have thought of that incident for years, but now that you're thinking of it, it's as vivid as the day it happened: the shame you felt as all the children laughed, the trauma of it.

What happened was that incident created a neural pathway (remember we said it only takes one incident if it's a high emotion one?) which believed: a) people will laugh at you and b) that's not safe for you, therefore c) you need to avoid that risk above all.

And that is the block to applying for the job (or one of them; there may be more).

So you tap using *They laughed at me in school that time I spilled the paint* as your tapping statement until it is a 0 of upset or another thought comes.

Once a tapping statement is a 0 of upset, go back to the next one above it and see what the score is now. It could now be also a 0 as you were working on its foundation issue, or at least be decreased.

And tap for that until it is a 0, via another thought/belief/memory if that comes up.

In this way you will process and eliminate all that stops you from applying for the job.

This might seem like a lot of work just to apply for one job, but:

- This all takes tens of minutes, not hours
- You can take breaks as needed; it doesn't need to be done together
- And it's not about applying for one job: it's about Blocking Beliefs that block you in many aspects of your life, and once you resolve them they are gone forever and you are free to pursue your choices.

See the image below for a visual representation of all of this:

Tapping Tree

Resistance to applying for the job

They'll only laugh at me

I won't get it, waste of time

The job will require too much travel

I can only do success-guaranteed things

Yep. Definitely too much travel. I won't apply after all

They laughed at me at school that time

My mother laughed when I said I wanted this career

Unless I apply band see if there is any flexibility about the travel requirements

8.4: Freeform Tapping

All that I have shared up until now is standard EFT / Tapping, and it works very well. But more and more I am coming to use a process I am calling Freeform Tapping, and I share that here.

What you do is to simply tap the points in turn, over and over, while you have a conversation with yourself about whatever is going on. You allow yourself to say whatever comes up, tapping a point for each statement.

Later, we go through all the various Blocking Beliefs you might hold: in other words, the beliefs which feel true, but are not, and which block you from going No-Contact. You can use this process for each one individually, but to give you an example here let's just use the overall topic that you want to go No-Contact but you feel that you cannot.

So a Freeform Tapping Session might go like this:

Karate Chop Point: I want to go No-Contact
Inner Eye: But I can't.
Outer Eye: I'm not allowed.
Under Eye: But I really want to.
Nose: I know, but I just can't.
Chin: But she hurts me so much.
Collarbone: I know, and it's so unfair.
Underarm: And she won't change.
Thumb: I know.
Index Finger: It's so frustrating.
Middle Finger: I know. It really is.
Ring Finger: She's so mean.
Little Finger: I know. It's why we need to go No-Contact.
Karate Chop: But we can't.
Inner Eye: Why can't we?
Outer Eye: We're not allowed.

Under Eye: Says who?
Nose: Says everyone.
Chin: But they don't know the truth.

Do you see how it works. You would just keep going until you find resolution. Now, the whole issue of Blocking Beliefs is huge, and this could take some time at this top level, and this is why we break it down further to individual Blocking Beliefs as you'll see in the next chapter.

We can also use Freeform Tapping with Committee Meetings: you simply allow both you and your Committee Member(s) to have their say as you tap. So this might look like the following. Note that I do not show the tapping points in this example as it might make the text hard to follow, but just know that you tap each subsequent point for each statement.

Say you have invited the Committee Member who believes good daughters don't abandon their mothers to come and talk with you. The tapping conversation might go as follows:

You: Can you tell me why you think No-Contact is an act of abandonment?
Committee Member: Because it clearly is! Walking away from her.
You: It certainly is walking away, but calling it 'abandoned'?
Committee Member: It's the only way to put it. Walking away from your own mother!
You: She hasn't acted as a mother.
Committee Member: Even so.

And so on until resolution.

How will you know when you have reached resolution?
You will feel it. It will just click, so to speak. It will be peaceful

and serene and just be right. It might well be a solution you would never have dreamed of, but it's so obvious now that you see it. Or it might be a solution you did think of, but weren't sure about. You know you're at resolution when you KNOW, in other words, know in your body rather than just in your head.

8.5 Tapping Scripts

If you would prefer more of a done-for-you process, I do offer Tapping Scripts for each of the Blocking Beliefs. Available in text, audio and/or video versions, you can find details at donm.info/htgnc-resources.

9
ALL ABOUT
BLOCKING BELIEFS

Remember we spoke of Blocking Beliefs? The beliefs you carry that block you from going No-Contact. Well, this is where we look at these, and help you realise that you do not have to believe them and certainly not to make your decisions based on them.

I did not create this list of Blocking Beliefs. Rather, they are all statements that have been shared with me, that have been the *but* in DONMs' self-talk. You can do the following list in any order that appeals.

9.1: Guilt

Before we dive into all the Blocking Beliefs, I need to speak here of guilt.

To judge from my correspondence, guilt is the number one block to going No-Contact, so obviously we need to resolve that.

The first thing to say is that the guilt is *real* but it's not *true*.

I say it's *real* because it is. It's there; you're feeling it and experiencing it. We're not trying to minimise or deny that, nor to invalidate you.

But I also say that the guilt is not *true* because it's not applicable. There is no need for guilt in this situation. Let me explain:

Guilt is our friend, helping to keep us in integrity, and thereby warning us if/when we do something wrong.

But sometimes it has incorrect information about

what is the wrong thing to do. In our example, your guilt – understandably – thinks that going No-Contact is wrong. It thinks this because of our societal story about mothers, and about your own mother's victim-playing and lies. In other words, it thinks you're doing something wrong because of the Blocking Beliefs.

In the following sections we are going to look at all the Blocking Beliefs, and hopefully erase them, and that should erase the guilt as you realise you're doing nothing wrong.

And we'll revisit the topic of guilt again after all that, to discuss if there is any left and how to manage it if so.

9.2: She might change

This is the eternal hope, isn't it? The hope that keeps us trapped in that hamster wheel of looking for her love, her approval, her kindness, her respect.

And, the thought goes (except it's not a conscious thought of course, but the buried belief): *If I just try harder, or be more patient, or [insert-magic-ingredient-here], she will change to be what I need and deserve. This time she'll be the mother we need her to be. This time she'll support us in our grief, applaud us in our success, be good company with no agenda. This time she'll accept us just as we are.*

This is completely understandable. We are all still that little girl desperately looking for her mother's love.

And, based on that, the fear is that if we go No-Contact now we will have missed out on that change. We gave up just before it would have worked. (Again, this belief would be deep and subconscious, not articulated.)

This is because of a natural human trait called the Sunk Cost Fallacy, where the more we have invested (time, money, energy, anything) in a project, the harder it is to accept that is has failed and to walk away. Understandable, but ultimately counter-productive.

Our logical mind might know that she is toxic and abusive and will not change, but our Little-Girl-Self is still hoping against hope.

This is completely understandable, but it does not serve us. This hope traps us in the toxic narcissistic dynamic.

The reality is that if your mother is narcissistic, she *will not* and *cannot* change.

And if, as we said above, you're wrong about her being narcissistic, well, as we said before, call her out on her behaviour, with or without ultimatums, and see if that works to change things, and when it doesn't, that is valuable information.

But I bet that you have tried and tried so much, and she still hasn't changed, so there is no reason to suppose she will change now. Don't forget, this whole dynamic works well for her. She has set it up to work for her. Okay, she might wish you were more biddable, and/or that you gave her more satisfaction when she gets her digs in, and/or that you paid her more attention. But the basic shape of the relationship is one that suits her. She has zero incentive to change, and will not. And your freedom lies in realising this, in giving up the hope that she will change, because this is the hope that traps you.

If this is a concern for you, by all means go back to Chapter 3.1 to see what we discussed on giving her one last chance.

Does this all make sense to you? Does it resonate with you? Do you feel the truth of this in your body?

If so, great.

If not, that's understandable. We spoke already of the

difference between knowing and KNOWING. To come to a place of KNOWING. I do invite you to play with Tapping, Freewriting and Committee Meetings to resolve this dilemma fully.

9.3: Giving her one last chance

Linked to the hope that she might yet change, is the urge or need to give her one last chance.

But, I offer you to consider that this is just a story you are telling yourself, a blocking belief you are carrying, and that you can let this story go.

The reality is that you have given your mother years and *years* of chances, and she has not changed any single time. You have let her off the hook over and over and over, and she has continued to take advantage of you and hurt you and abuse you. (And if you think you can't call it abuse: we discuss that shortly too.)

As we discussed already, you absolutely can give her another chance, either with or without an ultimatum. Doing this will give you all the information you need.

But it will take energy, and involve more pain and more rejection. You do not have to do this.

You do not owe your mother one last chance.

However, if this is a concern for you, by all means go back to Chapter 3.1 to see what we discussed on giving her one last chance.

Does this all make sense to you? Does it resonate with you? Do you feel the truth of this in your body?

If so great.

If not, that's understandable. We spoke already of the difference between knowing and KNOWING. To come to a place of KNOWING. I do invite you to play with Tapping,

Freewriting and Committee Meetings to resolve this dillemma fully.

9.4: Trauma bonding

Trauma bonding is a complex topic, but it can help us understand why we stay in this abusive relationship.

The first thing to understand about trauma bonding is that it is caused by something called *Intermittent Reinforcement Training*.

Intermittent Reinforcement means that rewards for behaviour are given at sporadic, random times.

So when you do something, you have no idea if this time it will lead to a reward or not. But it *might*! And this not-knowing is somehow more addictive than knowing you'll get a reward. It keeps us hooked on the hope, the sense of 'maybe this time'. Not consciously, of course, but that's what's going on all the same.

A classic example is slot-machines. They give intermittent rewards, on no particular schedule, and it seems that gambling addicts are addicted to the buzz of that moment after they pull the lever, but before the outcome is known. They're addicted to the *possibility*, in other words, rather than the *result*.

And abusers seem to know this dynamic. They give little rewards every so often, to keep us hooked into the relationship. I don't for one minute think they do this consciously, but they might feel us begin to pull away even a little, and so they drop a little reward to keep us trapped. And this reward might be as little as a kind word, maybe: it doesn't take much to hook those who are starved of affection and validation.

So, as you do this work, be aware that you will continue to feel a pull towards your mother, towards trying again, towards hoping for a better outcome. These are the patterns you know, and that are comfortable for you. And remember that your brain prefers to think the thoughts it already has programmed in, than create new thoughts.

Does this all make sense to you? Does it resonate with you? Do you feel the truth of this in your body?

If so, great.

If not, that's understandable. We spoke already of the difference between knowing and KNOWING. To come to a place of KNOWING. I do invite you to play with Tapping, Freewriting and Committee Meetings to resolve this dilemma fully.

9.5: What if she's not narcissistic?

Now, what if we're wrong about all of this? What if you're being completely unfair to her. What if she's not narcissistic after all?

And you know, she might not be. Most likely if you are reading this you are not qualified to diagnose her, and even if a therapist told you that your mother sounded narcissistic, that was not an official diagnosis. The person has to be assessed themselves, directly, for diagnosis of Narcissistic Personality Disorder.

So, your mother might not be narcissistic. You might be wrong about that. (As might I about my own mother. She was never officially diagnosed either and this is just my best guess.)

But what you're *not* wrong about is the way she has treated you all your life.

You're not wrong about the sly digs and the undermining and the cruel words and deeds, and the sabotage, and the selfishness and the invalidating and the gaslighting. You're not wrong about the contrived drama and the begrudgery of your successes even as she claims credit for them, and the tantrums when she doesn't get her own way, and the victim-playing whenever she is challenged, and the way she ignores boundaries like an invading army.

You're not wrong about the fact that she will never, ever admit there's anything wrong with what she's doing, and the way she'll never ever change. (Or, maybe, agree to change just to shut you up, and then ignore that promise.)

Narcissistic Personality Disorder is your best guess to explain all this. It is a label that seems to fit.

So even if we are wrong about her being narcissistic, her abusive behaviour still remains, and we are still fully entitled to protect ourselves from it.

But, you might ask, how do we know her behaviour even qualifies as abuse? We discuss this in the next section.

Does this all make sense to you? Does it resonate with you? Do you feel the truth of this in your body?

If so, great.

If not, that's understandable. We spoke already of the difference between knowing and KNOWING. To come to a place of KNOWING. I do invite you to play with Tapping, Freewriting and Committee Meetings to resolve this dilemma fully.

9.6: How do I know it's abuse?

How do you know your mother's behaviour qualifies as abuse?

Maybe – just as she always says – her behaviour is perfect and it's all your fault because you're just over-sensitive, over-dramatic, over-demanding, nothing ever pleases you, people have to walk on eggshells around you, etc., etc.

We could look up dictionary definitions of abuse, but you know, I don't think that will help. We don't have to label her behaviour as abuse in order to know it's not healthy or supportive or respectful.

You already know you're not happy in the relationship: that you come away from encounters with her exhausted and stressed and feeling really bad about yourself, that she undermines you and sabotages you and disrespects you and says nasty things to you and gaslights you. You already know all this, right?

So if this is not abuse, it is at the very least a completely dysfunctional dynamic that is impacting badly on you. She is mistreating you, and will not stop mistreating you.

However, be very clear: I'm sure it's abuse.

How do I know this? How can I say this without having ever met your mother?

Because you would not have been brought to the point of accessing this resource if she had been in any way a reasonable person. I promise you that happy women with good – or even adequate – relationships with their mothers do not take all the many steps – or indeed any of them – you took to find yourself accessing this resource.

Seriously, no daughter of a loving-but-flawed mother would ever get as far as reading these words now. Think of the journey that brought you to reading this information. That was a journey of hurt, and despair, and desperately seeking answers, wasn't it? That is the evidence of how bad this is.

I am confident to label all this as abuse, and I invite you to do so as well, and we will call it abuse going forward. If you are not happy with that word, just mentally substitute the phrase *bad treatment*, or whatever phrase works for you.

I also applaud you, and invite you to applaud yourself, for being so compassionate and fair-minded that even in the midst of this trauma and dysfunction, you are making sure to be fair to her.

Does this all make sense to you? Does it resonate with you? Do you feel the truth of this in your body?

If so, great.

If not, that's understandable. We spoke already of the difference between knowing and KNOWING. To come to a place of KNOWING. I do invite you to play with Tapping, Freewriting and Committee Meetings to resolve this dilemma fully.

9.7: She had a hard life

Trauma-bonding can manifest in various ways, and one big one is making excuses for our bad parents.

As children we need to believe our parents are good. They are our only survival option after all. Okay, nowadays if the authorities find out there is life-threatening abuse going on they will save us, so technically there are other options. But our primitive survival brain and our under-developed child brain doesn't know this. And so we need to believe in our parents' essential goodness.

BUT...

If they are mistreating us, how can that be? Good people wouldn't do this.

Bear in mind that we don't articulate this in actual discussion with ourselves. You might remember that we spoke earlier about implicit learning versus explicit learning, and how implicit learning is deeper and stronger, and we don't get to use our conscious minds to consider whether this learning is accurate.

This process of reconciling our need to believe our

parents are good on the one hand, and the fact they don't act in a good way on the other, is a classic example of this. We come to the conclusions without consciously articulating or evaluating them.

And so, we come up with excuses for them, reasons why they would behave like this, *and* be good people. We come up with ways that both those facts can be true.

And one logical solution is to believe that it's all our fault. We're a bad person so of course they have to treat us badly.

This is partly why DONMs and other abused children find self-esteem so challenging. Another reason is that, as well as us coming to the conclusion ourselves that the parent mistreats us because we're bad, the abusive parent also tells us this in so many words! So the message is subliminal *and* overt. We have no chance against that.

We DONMs can be extremely prone to minimising how bad our mothers are, and one way we do this is to excuse what she does by saying that she had a hard life.

This is one of the big excuses I hear from DONMs, as they try to resolve their cognitive dissonance around the whole crazy-making scenario.

And yep, she might well have had a hard life. People often do. And since Narcissistic Personality Disorder runs in families, then it's very possible she had a narcissistic parent herself, and as we know, that's a special kind of hell.

Plus, people go through all sorts of other stresses: poverty, illness, war, alcoholism in the family and so on.

Many, many people have hard lives, and your mother might well be one of them. She might not be, of course. She could be exaggerating for attention. However, for the purposes of this exercise we'll assume she is telling the truth.

So, okay, she had a hard life.

BUT ...

This is not a licence to turn around and treat others badly!

This statement is a classic case of a hidden *therefore:* She had a hard life, *therefore* I need to put up with the way she treats me.

When you explain it to yourself that bluntly, it doesn't seem to make as much sense, does it?

Most people who have had a hard life do their very best to make sure their own children don't have the same hard life.

Our narcissistic mothers use it as a way to excuse their behaviour.

We don't have to collaborate with her though in continuing this excuse.

Also, be aware that making excuses for an abusive parent is a classic symptom of trauma-bonding. As helpless children we are forced to try to resolve the cognitive dissonance between the fact she's abusing you on the one hand, and your need to think of her as a good person on the other, and blaming her behaviour on her own trauma is a very elegant way of doing that.

That was the solution then, and it worked. But it is a problem now if this belief forces us to continue to put up with the bad treatment.

So, we need to realise that even if she had a hard life, that does not excuse anything she does to us.

Her having a hard life (if she did) is a classic case of TBI: True But Irrelevant.

It may be true, but it has no bearing on the current circumstances.

Does this all make sense to you? Does it resonate with you? Do you feel the truth of this in your body?

If so, great.

If not, that's understandable. We spoke already of the difference between knowing and KNOWING. To come to a place of KNOWING. I do invite you to play with Tapping, Freewriting and Committee Meetings to resolve this dilemma fully.

9.8: She's not that bad

Another way we can minimise her behaviour is to say, to ourselves, Ah well she's not that bad.

And you know, she might not be. Now that I have spent all these years working with and communicating with other DONMs, I can safely say that my own mother was very mild on the spectrum of narcissistic nastiness.

But mild by narcissistic standards is still awful by loving and compassionate standards.

Also, we can tend to minimise her behaviour. This is partly because it's all we know, and partly because we need to minimise it for our own sanity in a way.

And saying, She's not that bad, is the way we do that.

How bad is bad enough? How bad is acceptable?

I argue that any bad is too bad, and I invite you to consider that you might accept that too.

Okay, for sure, don't abandon someone for normal human foibles. We're not looking for perfection here. Mothers aren't robots. Even kind, loving, compassionate mothers have their moments, and their bad habits and so on.

But that's not what we're talking about here. You wouldn't have been brought to the point of receiving this information if you had a normally flawed decent mother.

I invite you to read back on your *Greatest Hits* list any time you find yourself thinking that she isn't that bad, and this is the reason for its creation. Also, I include below a list of the differences between real mothers and narcissistic mothers, for you to see on which side your own mother falls. You might use list as inspiration to add to the Greatest Hits too.

The difference between real mothers and narcissistic mothers

Because we normalise our narcissistic mother's treatment of us, we can fail to realise exactly how bad it is, or to even know what kind mothers do. Here is a list of some ways where real mothers are different from narcissistic mothers.

- Where real mothers build us up, narcissistic mothers knock us down. They either do it deliberately, for the pleasure of that. Or just carelessly, as collateral damage to their own wishes.
- Real mothers provide a soft place to fall when their daughters are down and weary. Ours begrudgingly provide a barren concrete slab. Or maybe a mattress of barbed wire, for the fun of adding to our misery.
- Real mothers see themselves and their daughters as being on the same side. Our mothers see us as the opposition.
- Real mothers enjoy our company. Narcissistic mothers enjoy our attention.
- Real mothers respect us. Narcissistic mothers reject us.
- Real mothers see their daughters' beauty and applaud it. Ours will make sure we know all our flaws.
- Real mothers want their daughters to fulfil all their potential. Ours do not want us outshining them. Unless they want us to do well as a reflection on them. Often they can have both of these desires ('Don't outshine me but do well to make me look good') and so we're in a no-win situation there.

- Real mothers know they are responsible for their own lives and their own happiness. Narcissistic mothers try to make us responsible for those things.
- Real mothers know, accept and even rejoice in the fact that we are separate people with our own opinions, tastes and life paths. Narcissistic mothers get offended if we think or live differently from them.
- Real mothers see us as us. Narcissistic mothers don't really see us as real people at all, but rather their own reflections.
- Real mothers rejoice in their daughters' successes. Narcissistic mothers resent them. And/or hijack them.
- Real mothers mourn for our sorrows. Narcissistic mothers relish the drama of them.
- Real mothers delight in their daughters. Ours delight in what we can do for them.
- Real mothers are interested in their daughters' lives. Ours have no interest in anything outside themselves, except to the extent that our lives can reflect well on them.
- Real mothers are mostly kind. Ours are completely selfish.
- Real mothers are warm. Narcissistic mothers are cold. Except for the heat of rage.
- Real mothers hold us in their hearts. Narcissistic mothers hold us hostage.
- Real mothers can be testy and cranky and short-tempered at times. Our mothers are downright nasty most of the time.
- Real mothers are willing to discuss and compromise. Narcissistic mothers invented 'my way or the highway' .
- Real mothers look for the win-win. Narcissistic mothers insist on the 'I win'.
- Real mothers love their daughters. Our mothers love what their daughters can do for them.

- Real mothers can be annoying, with foibles and faults. Narcissistic mothers are emotionally and psychologically toxic.

Does this all make sense to you? Does it resonate with you? Do you feel the truth of this in your body?

If so, great.

If not, that's understandable. We spoke already of the difference between knowing and KNOWING. To come to a place of KNOWING. I do invite you to play with Tapping, Freewriting and Committee Meetings to resolve this dilemma fully.

9.9: How do I know it's bad enough to justify going No-Contact?

Okay, you might say, she definitely is that bad. But is she bad enough to justify going No-Contact?

This question implies that you have to justify going No-Contact, that there is some arbiter who will decide when you're allowed to leave her. That there is some level of abuse (you might struggle to use the word 'abuse', and if so, go back to Chapter 9.6) that you have to reach before No-Contact is permitted. That there is some higher authority who will allow you, or not allow you, to go No-Contact.

And this isn't true. There's no government body or other authority who gets to decide this. The only one who can decide it is you.

You might hold the belief (perhaps without even realising it) that it is unfair of you to go No-Contact the way she currently treats you. This is because the current situation is all you know, and you normalise it and minimise the bad events.

The big issue is: how do you feel in this relationship? Does it enhance you or diminish you? Do you come away from seeing her feeling energised and happy, or depleted and down in yourself? (For sure, you can feel depleted in a healthy relationship if you are supporting the person through a tough time. But that is not what we are talking about here. We are talking about feeling depleted after every encounter.)

Does she support you or undermine you? Does she respect you or disrespect you? Is she interested in you as a person or only as an audience?

I invite you to give yourself permission to make your happiness a priority in your own life, and to know that it's reasonable to cut out things and people that don't contribute to that, and even more so, things and people who actively sabotage your happiness.

Does this all make sense to you? Does it resonate with you? Do you feel the truth of this in your body?

If so, great.

If not, that's understandable. We spoke already of the difference between knowing and KNOWING. To come to a place of KNOWING. I do invite you to play with Tapping, Freewriting and Committee Meetings to resolve this dilemma fully.

9.10: I need to wait for her to do one more really bad action

This belief -- that you need to wait for her to do just one more really bad thing in order to be allowed to go No-Contact -- is related to the previous one in that it contains the belief that she hasn't been bad enough so far.

The word 'allow' is powerful. I use it deliberately. And it's to show that we are looking to some authority outside ourselves for permission to go No-Contact, and we feel that this outside authority will need one more bit of evidence before permitting it.

Also, often Narcissistic Mothers, especially those ones on the milder end of the scale, will never do one really bad thing. My own mother never did anything proactively and deliberately nasty. All her abuse came from her reacting to my expression of my needs (e.g. for support during a miscarriage). There were lots of small things: death by a thousand cuts rather than one big sabre. And we are allowed to free ourselves from that too.

Which of course, is totally understandable. No-Contact is a huge step, and a terrifyingly final one, with all sorts of implications. No wonder it's scary to consider taking that final decision.

You don't need to make the No-Contact decision now, or ever. Or, if you do decide you want to go No-Contact, you don't need to actually do it just yet. If you're not yet sure, I invite you to wait until you are finished with this resource so you are armed as best you can be with perspectives and tools and information and resources, before going No-Contact.

But regardless of what decisions you make around No-Contact, I offer you to realise that she *has* been bad enough, for long enough, that you do not need her to do one more thing, or one really bad thing, to justify your right to go No-Contact.

I further invite you to realise that the only one who gets to allow you or forbid you any action, is you. You are the boss of your life.

I invite you to give yourself the permission you need to do what's right for you.

Another aspect to this issue is your hope that if she does one really bad thing, even *she* will have to realise that No-Contact was justified. That will never happen. She will never admit that she has done wrong, and your freedom lies in allowing yourself to know that. As a narcissist she will never admit any wrong-doing, not even to herself.

Does this all make sense to you? Does it resonate with you? Do you feel the truth of this in your body?

If so, great.

If not, that's understandable. We spoke already of the difference between knowing and KNOWING. To come to a place of KNOWING. I do invite you to play with Tapping, Freewriting and Committee Meetings to resolve this dilemma fully.

9.11: She'll miss me too much

We will speak more of this in a coming section on how she might react if/when you go No-Contact, but for now let's talk about your believing you are responsible for making sure she doesn't end up missing you and being sad because of that.

As we already said, narcissistic mothers are very good at making us feel responsible for their happiness and well-being.

They're wrong. We're not responsible for those things.

As adults, our NMs are responsible for their own lives and their own happiness. They have no right to dump the responsibility for their happiness onto you.

AND ...

Let us not forget that you wouldn't be considering No-Contact if she had treated you half-way decently. This situation is none of your choosing, but is one of her making.

So the statement that she might miss you falls into the

category of TBI: True But Irrelevant. She might well miss you, but it's not your problem.

Plus, when we speak of her missing us, don't forget that she's not missing us the way we miss people we lose.

Rather, she's missing her chew-toy, her source of narcissistic supply.

The analogy I always use, and that you might have read from me before, is that of a cat who brings in a mouse, and the owner rescues the mouse, and the cat is frantically looking everywhere for the mouse, miaowing piteously, obviously upset.

There is no doubt that the cat is genuinely missing the mouse.

But the cat is missing the mouse as prey, not as someone to have a loving mutually respectful and mutually supportive relationship with.

This is what is happening when our narcissistic mother misses us, and we are under zero obligation to give the mouse back to the cat so it can continue to torment it and eventually kill it.

We can feel sorry for the fact she misses us, but to do so from a safe distance. And we don't even have to feel sorry for her, frankly. It is no reflection on us if we don't. An abuser lost access to her victim, is what has happened, and the fact that the abuser is sad about that, is not our problem.

If she'd wanted you to hang around, she should have been nicer to you.

Does this all make sense to you? Does it resonate with you? Do you feel the truth of this in your body?

If so, great.

If not, that's understandable. We spoke already of the difference between knowing and KNOWING. To come to a place of KNOWING. I do invite you to play with Tapping, Freewriting and Committee Meetings to resolve this dilemma fully.

9.12: No-Contact would hurt her so much

It might. That is the reality.

It'll certainly hurt her pride. Narcissists hate rejection with a passion, and here you are rejecting her. And of course they think they're so wonderful, and that they're the bee's knees, and here you are telling them in effect that they're really not all that. That's going to hurt.

But I struggle to think of any other way it'll hurt her. It's not like normal people losing family members. Yes, it'll irritate her and annoy her and frustrate her and infuriate her and whatever other synonyms we can find for such emotions. It might well embarrass her as she has to find excuses to tell people why you're not around, excuses that put all the blame on you and none on her of course.

Again, to revisit our earlier metaphor, think of how a cat is distressed if you confiscate a mouse it brought home. The cat is missing its prey, and your mother's distress would be of the same calibre.

But it won't hurt her in the normal sense. She doesn't love you and so she won't be bereaved from your absence.

Let's accept, for argument's sake, that she does miss you. (She doesn't, but this is just a thought experiment.) So, say she does miss you and is sad and so on. Even so, it is not your responsibility to protect her from that sadness at the cost of your own sanity and well-being and happiness and self-esteem and joy and peace. And that is what she demands: *Keep me happy despite how much I hurt you.*

You have zero obligation to do this, and I hope you can see that.

Does this all make sense to you? Does it resonate with

you? Do you feel the truth of this in your body?

If so, great.

If not, that's understandable. We spoke already of the difference between knowing and KNOWING. To come to a place of KNOWING. I do invite you to play with Tapping, Freewriting and Committee Meetings to resolve this dilemma fully.

9.13: She depends on me

We spoke in Chapter 5 about why you might choose to stay in contact with your Narcissistic Mother, for example how you might be trapped in the relationship by living with her.

But even without that, you might find that you are – to a greater or lesser extent – responsible for some or all of her care: organising medical appointments, dealing with landlords or garden maintenance companies and so on.

Narcissists are very good at creating strategic helplessness. They make you feel (and even be) responsible for all sorts of situations that they are well able to take care of themselves.

Now, this situation is somewhat complicated by the fact that your Narcissistic Mother may well be at an age where she does start to need help and where you, as her adult daughter, might be expected to take on some of these burdens.

Obviously only you can decide on the realities of this, but I invite you to consider the following:

- The first is that even if she genuinely does need help, you might be able to arrange it from a distance rather than being personally involved.
- The second is that if your mother continues to be nasty to you, she cannot expect you to look after her. She should

have thought of her needs before being so horrible, and that you are completely justified in walking away. If you didn't exist, or had died, other arrangements would have had to be made, and those arrangements can be made now.

• And the third is that if you cannot delegate her care, and genuinely cannot come up with any other options, you can still go No-Contact otherwise. Strictly this would be called Low Contact, but the same principles apply in that you are protecting yourself from her abuse.

Does this all make sense to you? Does it resonate with you? Do you feel the truth of this in your body?

If so, great.

If not, that's understandable. We spoke already of the difference between knowing and KNOWING. To come to a place of KNOWING. I do invite you to play with Tapping, Freewriting and Committee Meetings to resolve this dilemma fully.

9.14: Is No-Contact abusing her back?

Short answer: No.

Longer answer: No-Contact is not something you are doing *to* her. It is something you are doing (if you choose) *for* yourself. Yes, it will have fallout for her, but that is not abuse, it is natural consequences.

One of the big lies our narcissistic mother teaches us is that we have to protect her from the consequences of her actions, and it's not surprising we believe it and live it. But I offer you to let this belief go.

If you were to call her names, or physically attack her, or

similar, that would be abuse. Simply removing yourself is not abuse, not one bit. You are entitled to protect yourself from people who treat you badly.

Now, there is no doubt that she will spin it as you abusing her, but as we know from all the years of invalidating and gaslighting, the way your Narcissistic Mother says things are, is very rarely the way things actually are. You do not have to buy into her narrative.

Does this all make sense to you? Does it resonate with you? Do you feel the truth of this in your body?

If so, great.

If not, that's understandable. We spoke already of the difference between knowing and KNOWING. To come to a place of KNOWING. I do invite you to play with Tapping, Freewriting and Committee Meetings to resolve this dilemma fully.

9.15: I should look for the good in her

DONMs have said this to me several times, and I do get it. We seem to spend all our time dissing our mother, and talking, or thinking, about all her bad traits. Surely there should be good there, if we just look for it.

Years ago, long long before I ever realised about Narcissistic Personality Disorder, I thought the same, and I worked really hard to think of my mother's good traits.

And honestly, I could find none. Well, one: she was an extremely good cook and baker. Credit where it's due. But that didn't impact on her relationship with others; that wasn't a personality trait. And in fairness, she spoke to me about the facts of life/puberty, etc. very clearly and age-appropriately. Many DONMs, I now know, are never told anything.

But apart from those two very low-bar examples, I could find no redeeming features for her. She was never kind, she was not a good conversationalist (unless you were fascinated by her specialist topic: herself), she wasn't adult or mature, she was lazy, etc ...

So, I could have condemned myself to constantly looking for the good in her but that would have been an exercise in futility, and a huge time suck and energy suck.

Instead I just accepted the fact and made my decisions accordingly. My decision at the time, for possibly two decades, was to just keep trying to get on with her, and put up with her and endure it all.

But say you do find good in her, and that's very possible. She could be good company, or very witty, or great at teaching you new skills.

What I suggest is that this doesn't matter.

If she treats you badly, then any good points on top of that are irrelevant. Spreading jam (jelly in the USA) on top of poison doesn't make it any less poisonous.

Just because she does some good things does not cancel out the narcissistic abuse she doles out, and you don't have to think it does. You don't have to put up with abuse because there are some good traits.

Another way to look at it is to use one of the most powerful phrases I know: TBI. This stands for: True But Irrelevant.

It's the way we can acknowledge something is true, but also that it does not change the main point of the discussion. And your mother having some good traits is, in the context of you freeing yourself from her abuse, TBI.

Does this all make sense to you? Does it resonate with you? Do you feel the truth of this in your body?

If so, great.

If not, that's understandable. We spoke already of the difference between knowing and KNOWING. To come to a place of KNOWING. I do invite you to play with Tapping, Freewriting and Committee Meetings to resolve this dilemma fully.

9.16: But she's nice sometimes

One dynamic that might confuse you mightily is the fact that your mother might be nice sometimes.

This is very confusing, so that you don't know where you stand with her, and you don't know how you are allowed to react to her. (I use the word 'allowed' advisedly as all of this is us believing there is some other/outside authority.)

It is no accident that she is nice sometimes.

There's a process called Intermittent Reinforcement Training. It's where the trainer gives intermittent, random, rewards. Well, this is exactly what all abusers do. I don't think for one minute that they do this consciously, but they are watching your reactions and will drop a little kindness or treat when they feel they need to in order to keep you trapped.

In this way, the occasional kindnesses do not cancel out the abuse, but rather *they are an integral part of the abuse*.

So you do not have to feel guilty about leaving a relationship in which someone has been nice sometimes. In a healthy relationship, people are nice nearly all the time, not just sometimes. For sure, they can be cranky, and tired, and have their moments. But that will be the exception, rather than the niceness being the exception as is the case with abusers.

The abusers can use their occasional kindnesses to trap you further: when you try to call them on their bad behaviour, they may say: *'But look at X, Y, and Z that I did for you!'*

My own parents were very good at this one and it confused me completely and always shut me up. But I didn't know then what I know now: that doing nice things for people you supposedly love is the baseline! It's a given. It doesn't give a licence to abuse. It's not a get-out-of-jail-free card to do what you like the rest of the time. Relationships are not a bank account where if you deposit enough favours you can do an equal amount of abuse.

Nobody should be abusing you, full stop.

Does this all make sense to you? Does it resonate with you? Do you feel the truth of this in your body?

If so, great.

If not, that's understandable. We spoke already of the difference between knowing and KNOWING. To come to a place of KNOWING. I do invite you to play with Tapping, Freewriting and Committee Meetings to resolve this dilemma fully.

9.17: But I owe her so much

This one comes up a lot for DONMs looking to go No-Contact. Either they say it to themselves, as they think of all that their mother did for them, or, if they don't, you may be sure their narcissistic mother will say it to them: 'After all I've done for you!'

And it's very possible that their mother *has* done lots for them, often financially.

One example that springs to mind is that the narcissistic mother had just paid a fortune for the DONM's wedding, and the DONM wanted to go No-Contact but she couldn't do it right now, for that exact reason. It would be so ungrateful. The narcissistic mother would be so angry at this.

However:

It's not surprising that the help that is given is often financial. If a narcissistic mother is well off, she's quite likely to use that money to help her daughter. But that help always comes with strings attached: the strings of allowing the narcissistic mother to continue to behave exactly as she wishes without attempts at boundaries.

And it's completely understandable that the daughter will feel obligation towards her mother because of this.

And that is precisely the point of the help, of the gift.

It's not a gift, it's more manipulation. Or, sowing the seeds for future manipulation.

The fact is that nothing obliges you to put up with abuse, and that you are perfectly entitled to remove yourself from anyone who abuses you. And the fact that she recently paid for your expensive wedding or provided other financial help does not change that one bit.

Now of course your narcissistic mother will not see it that way, especially as she does not admit the abuse in the first place. She will absolutely spin a narrative about how her ungrateful daughter took all that money and then just abandoned her. And it will sound plausible to others, as, without the original basic fact of ongoing and unrelenting abuse, the situation does sound bad.

But you know the truth about the situation, and that is the only truth that matters. And we will be exploring later how to deal with others' opinions, others who have heard your narcissistic mother's side of the story.

For now, I invite you to make the decision that your mother cannot buy the right to abuse you. That's not for sale.

Okay, but what if the help was more personal than just money. What if she was there for you during an illness or other difficult time?

Even so. That does not give her a licence to abuse you. And what we are talking about, don't forget, is you protecting yourself from abuse, and all else is irrelevant.

Maybe, if this is right for you, the fact that she has helped you might justify giving her one more chance, one discussion about resolving your relationship in a way that works for you both. We spoke above of how that works out, but it might be worth your while to try it now, or again, to know you are doing what you feel is right regarding the help your mother gave. Or, you might just allow yourself to know that you have already done all this.

Okay, but what about the fact she gave you life and raised you and fed and clothed and educated you? (To whatever extent she did all that.)

It was her choice to have a baby, and all that came from that was her responsibility, both legally and morally. I argue that you owe her nothing for that. And certainly you do not owe her to passively accept her abuse of you for your whole life. That is not part of the contract at all.

Either way, the bottom line is that, as we have said many times but which bears repeating now, nothing means you have to put up with being abused. And that includes anything good that she has done.

If she would change now, and treat you well going forward, then maybe you could draw a line under all that happened before. That would be your choice for sure, not an obligation.

But that is not the situation we are dealing with, because the abuse is ongoing, and she is refusing to accept she is doing anything wrong and therefore refusing to change, and therefore unless you remove yourself the abuse will continue forever.

And the occasional crumbs of help do not change that.

Does this all make sense to you? Does it resonate with you? Do you feel the truth of this in your body?

If so, great.

If not, that's understandable. We spoke already of the difference between knowing and KNOWING. To come to a place of KNOWING. I do invite you to play with Tapping, Freewriting and Committee Meetings to resolve this dilemma fully.

9.18: I need to be a good person

If you find yourself thinking this, I invite you to explore using Freewriting or Tapping all your hidden *therefores* beneath this thought.

My thoughts are that being a good person means that you don't abuse others. It doesn't mean that you have to allow yourself to be constantly abused.

This worry is framed in other ways too.

I need to do the right thing.

Again, there are hidden *therefores* and assumptions behind this statement. How do you know what the right thing is? Right according to whom? Who gets to be the boss of what's right? Again, Freewriting and Tapping will help you resolve this, but in the meantime I offer you to realise that there is nothing wrong with protecting yourself from an abuser.

I need to be the bigger person

Again, I invite you to explore what this actually means to you, and where this belief comes from, and what it actually means.

To my mind, the phrase 'be the bigger person' is the biggest con-job going. It's often said to you by others, and we'll be exploring this later on in this resource.

Does this all make sense to you? Does it resonate with

you? Do you feel the truth of this in your body?

If so, great.

If not, that's understandable. We spoke already of the difference between knowing and KNOWING. To come to a place of KNOWING. I do invite you to play with Tapping, Freewriting and Committee Meetings to resolve this dilemma fully.

9.19: I should be strong enough to put up with her

This is one I hear often from DONMs. They feel that it is a failing in them that they cannot endure their mother's treatment of them. The reality is that it is a failing in their mother that she cannot treat people right.

Again, it is your mother forcing this dilemma. As already discussed, she will not change. So your only options are to put up with the treatment, or to remove yourself from her.

Don't forget that the word 'should' is always suspicious and should (ha!) be analysed to see if the 'should' statement is true.

I invite you to consider that there is zero obligation on you to force yourself to be strong enough to put up with abuse (or bad treatment, if you don't want to label it as abuse). There are no medals going for this, no awards, nothing except a lifetime of being someone else's victim.

You do not need to do this, and I invite you to honour yourself more than that. You deserve much much more.

I invite you to give yourself permission to stop being someone's punching bag.

Healthy relationships do not require endurance.

Does this all make sense to you? Does it resonate with you? Do you feel the truth of this in your body?

If so, great.

If not, that's understandable. We spoke already of the difference between knowing and KNOWING. To come to a place of KNOWING. I do invite you to play with Tapping, Freewriting and Committee Meetings to resolve this dilemma fully.

9.20: Is No-Contact just running away?

In a way this is the other side of the coin of the previous question about being strong enough to put up with it.

It's a good question of course. It does feel like running away doesn't it? It can feel like a selfish, sulking, pouting, immature 'I'll show her!' kind of a response. And the addition of the word 'just' in this context makes it sound like a whim, a frivolous decision.

And it might be, of course. If your motivation is a sulky immature one, then yes, I guess that would be true.

I would venture to guess though that that is such a rare reaction. I've certainly never come across it in all these years of communicating with thousands of DONMs. And certainly one who is asking that question, who is worrying about being like that, is not doing it. That immature one would not be second-guessing herself like this.

Don't forget that you are considering No-Contact only when you have tried everything else, and none of it has worked.

So, it's not a case of running away rather than staying to deal with the situation. It's running away (although I'll come back to that phrase in a minute), after having spent years trying, and failing, to deal with the situation. It's running away after years of being the only one trying to heal the situation while your mother went on gaily in her own selfish way. It's running away when you sadly, but realistically, acknowledge that the situation cannot be resolved, and certainly not by you.

And therefore, it is not running away. That is a very emotive and self-judgmental term. It has implications of immaturity and abandoning ship at the first sign of trouble.

I would sooner say that what you are doing is to calmly and realistically accept that this situation cannot be solved, that you deserve to be free of abuse, and therefore you are removing yourself from the clutches of an abuser.

And if someone – probably you to yourself – says, *Ah that's ridiculous, you're just spinning it so you feel better about it.* What then?

Spin is inaccurate slanting of a situation to put it in a favourable light. In this case I believe you would be looking at the facts clearly rather than spinning. She does abuse you. You have spent years trying to sort it out. You have consistently failed. You do realise now that because she's narcissistic she cannot and will not change. You realise you deserve to be treated well and not abused. Therefore you have no choice but to remove yourself from the situation.

That's the reality of being the daughter of a narcissistic mother. It's not spin. If anything, the statement that you are running away rather than dealing with the situation is spin. Negative spin, informed by the years of psychological abuse which makes you see everything from her angle and nothing from your own.

So, no, I don't think it's running away rather than dealing with it. I think it's calmly and appropriately walking away from an abuser.

Does this all make sense to you? Does it resonate with

you? Do you feel the truth of this in your body?

If so, great.

If not, that's understandable. We spoke already of the difference between knowing and KNOWING. To come to a place of KNOWING. I do invite you to play with Tapping, Freewriting and Committee Meetings to resolve this dilemma fully.

9.21: You can't just dump your mother!

This is one of Society's beliefs; indeed, one of Society's strongest rules.

For a start, the word 'dump' is very emotive. It has implications of abandonment and throwing away. It assumes immoral behaviour.

And I didn't deliberately use the word 'dump' merely to shoot it down. This is the word that DONMs use to me as they work through their own relationship with their mother. So I use the word deliberately as dumping is what it feels like to DONMs.

Plus, note the use of the word 'just'. This is a word also used by DONMs, and in this context it means that the dumping is done on a whim. *Bored today, think I'll dump my mother for something to do*, kind of thing.

Again, I invite you to look at this belief and see if it's true.

You can't just dump your mother? Sez who?

I don't mean this flippantly. I genuinely ask you to look at the source of this statement, and see if it's true.

Society says you can't dump your mother. But as we've already discussed, Society is frequently wrong.

And we are not talking about a situation where it is you,

on some whim, callously abandoning this sweet, wonderful woman who nurtures you and loves you. We are discussing you (if you choose) removing yourself from someone who consistently runs you down, undermines you and makes you feel bad. It's not dumping her at all, in the pejorative sense of dumping; rather it is protecting yourself.

Does this all make sense to you? Does it resonate with you? Do you feel the truth of this in your body?

If so, great.

If not, that's understandable. We spoke already of the difference between knowing and KNOWING. To come to a place of KNOWING. I do invite you to play with Tapping, Freewriting and Committee Meetings to resolve this dilemma fully.

9.22: What if she can't help it?

Okay, you might be thinking: Even if I accept that she's abusive, surely if she has Narcissistic Personality Disorder, she can't help being how she is. And if that's the case, then I shouldn't blame her for it, and shouldn't therefore go No-Contact.

Narcissistic people are not insane. They are fully in control of their actions. Narcissistic Personality Disorder is not a defence in court the way insanity is for example; you are still considered responsible in the way an insane person is not.

Narcissists absolutely know what they're doing; they just don't care.

The best way I can understand it – and I could be wrong of course, not being in their minds – is to consider the way I feel about yesterday's newspaper. I don't hold it any ill-will, but neither do I care about its feelings. I got value from it yesterday when I read it, but its value is gone now, and so today without a thought I throw it in the recycling bin. It has served my purposes and my purposes are the only ones that matter in this dynamic. I do not even consider how the newspaper feels about it.

However, I am fully in control of my actions. I can choose not to bin the paper. I could put the newspaper in a comfy spot on the sofa. But I don't, because I don't consider it to have any needs or concerns and it doesn't suit me to do that. My desire for a tidy house, without newspapers on the sofa, is way more important than anything about the newspaper.

In the same way narcissists don't care about how we feel. They don't consider us real people, or if they do, it doesn't matter. Our needs and desires are of no more importance than a newspaper's needs and desires. The only desires that matter are theirs.

So she fully has a choice about how she acts in the same way that I fully have a choice about binning the newspaper.

But here's the thing: I don't really have a practical choice between binning the newspaper on the one hand or cherishing it on the other because there's only one sensible option out of those. Cherishing the newspaper would be absurd and ridiculous and even a bit silly, wouldn't it? And even if someone insisted to me that the newspaper was sentient and had feelings, I'd think they were ridiculous, because my world view and my knowledge is absolutely that newspapers don't have feelings, and that out-of-date newspapers don't matter, and certainly don't matter as much as my desire for a tidy house. So I *could* make either decision, theoretically, but there is only one reasonable and realistic option - to bin the newspaper.

And in the same way the narcissist's world view and 'knowledge' is that nothing matters except her own desires. So no more than I can be persuaded to take the newspaper's feelings into account, she cannot be persuaded to take other people's feelings into account.

So it's a paradox. She can help it *and* she can't. Or, said another way, she can help it, but there is no good reason for her to do so.

So, if she cannot help it in any real sense in her world view, does that mean you have to put up with it? Surely if she can't help doing it, you shouldn't make her face consequences for it? We don't hold toddlers responsible for their actions, after all, because we know that they cannot in any real sense be responsible for what they do. We just sigh and get the cloth to wash the crayon off the wall, or whatever.

My answer to that is this: A tiger cannot help being a killer. We don't blame her or judge her for that. But we make very sure to stay out of her way. We can understand the tiger and protect ourselves at the same time. And we fully have the right to protect ourselves. We're not obliged to let the tiger kill us in order to satisfy her nature. Of course we're not. We're fully entitled to preserve our own life.

And so, when it comes to narcissists I think we can understand what's going on for them, and maybe even sympathise, but to do so from a safe distance.

The fact that she cannot, at some level, help it, does not mean we have to passively accept abuse. Not one bit. Even in my example above of the toddler writing on the wall -- we would make sure going forward to keep the crayons safely out of their hands, right? We don't blame, but we don't facilitate either.

Does this all make sense to you? Does it resonate with you? Do you feel the truth of this in your body?

If so, great.

If not, that's understandable. We spoke already of the difference between knowing and KNOWING. To come to a place of **KNOWING**. I do invite you to play with Tapping, Freewriting and Committee Meetings to resolve this dilemma fully.

9.23: I need to forgive her

Whether from a Christian perspective, or societal one, DONMs can hold the belief that they have to forgive their narcissistic mothers.

Usually forgiveness is given after the other person has apologised and repented. As we know, narcissists never do that. So the first step towards forgiveness doesn't even happen, and I would argue that we are under zero obligation to forgive our narcissistic mothers even by Society's rules in this case. Luke 17:3 Ministries gives biblical quotes to back this up, for Christians.

The fact is that narcissists never genuinely apologise. They might give a fauxpology, where they say they are sorry you feel that way, or similar, but never a genuine apology, and never acknowledge they did anything wrong, nor feel any need to change their behaviour. So, you forgiving them is just enabling them to keep abusing you.

Is this right? Is this continued abuse what you want? Is this what you deserve? If that is what you mean by forgiveness, I invite you to let that belief go.

Or does 'forgiveness' mean to let go of your anger and hurt? If so, then great. This is something you are doing for you, and it can only be good. But I think this kind of forgiveness should be as a *result* of your healing, rather than something you must force yourself to do. I don't think that you should feel bad if you cannot yet let go of the anger and hurt. Those feelings are messengers as we said, and maybe they still need to be heard. EFT / Tapping can help you process those feelings and let them go.

Or does forgiveness mean that you wish her well going forward, but that you do so from a safe distance, and never let her hurt you again? If so, I celebrate that for you.

Does forgiveness mean that you get over what she did, and let her carry on the way she is? That is how my mother always meant forgiveness when she'd say crossly that I was very unforgiving. I think, no. It cannot mean that. What do you think? That would be good to Freewrite about.

I do think though, categorically, that forgiving does not equal continuing to put up with abuse. So in this case it is a side-issue to going No-Contact, rather than something you have to resolve before deciding to go No-Contact.

Does this all make sense to you? Does it resonate with you? Do you feel the truth of this in your body?

If so, great.

If not, that's understandable. We spoke already of the difference between knowing and KNOWING. To come to a place of KNOWING. I do invite you to play with Tapping, Freewriting and Committee Meetings to resolve this dilemma fully.

9.24: I need to honour her

This is a huge issue for Christian DONMs who obviously want to be true to the tenets of their faith, but this can conflict with their need to protect themselves.

I do not speak from my own knowledge in this context, as I am not qualified in any way to do so, but I share two very valuable perspectives.

The first is a website Luke 17:3 Ministries. It is run by Sister Renee and describes itself as:

We are a Bible-based and Holy Ghost-inspired sisterhood for those who seek support in developing self-esteem, setting boundaries and limits, forgiveness, Godly confrontation, recognizing and cutting ties with reprobates, healing, and rejoicing in the peace and love of the Lord, our Father.

There is a wealth of biblically-sourced information on this site, and I offer you to read it.

One very valuable perspective I picked up from it was that by going No-Contact you are honouring your abusive parents by removing their opportunity to sin in this specific way.

I hope that this information will help you realise that honouring does not mean to allow someone to abuse you.

Does this all make sense to you? Does it resonate with you? Do you feel the truth of this in your body?

If so, great.

If not, that's understandable. We spoke already of the difference between knowing and KNOWING. To come to a place of KNOWING. I do invite you to play with Tapping, Freewriting and Committee Meetings to resolve this dilemma fully.

9.25: What if I regret it later?

What if you regret going No-Contact?

What if your mother dies without you ever being in touch with her again, and the guilt and the regret overwhelm you? Could you live with yourself in that case? That would be such a burden to carry for the rest of your life.

This is a question that I think every DONM has to face. Here are my thoughts on that:

Don't forget: if you had a normal, healthy, loving

relationship with a normal, healthy, loving mother, you wouldn't even be having this dilemma. You would simply stay in contact with each other, enjoying each other's company, for all the years you have left.

The fact you are even having this dilemma says it all about the dysfunction of the relationship.

You can use Tapping and/or Freewriting to ease this fear of regret now, so that this fear isn't stopping you from making your No-Contact decision.

And if the time comes that your mother has died without you being in contact, and you do have regret at the time, you can use Tapping to ease the regret in the moment, and/or freewrite a dialogue with your regret at the time.

In addition, here is another perspective:

What if you use this fear of regret to stop you going No-Contact, and at the end of your life, you regret *that* decision?

This is your only life as the person you are today on this Earth (reincarnation supposes a different you, and a heavenly afterlife precludes you being in this body living this life). You deserve to live the best life possible, and that does not include being consistently abused.

There will almost inevitably come a time when you are old, and lying on your own death bed, and all choices and options are now closed to you, and all you have left is your perspective on your own life, and whether it was a life well-lived.

And the question is: is it well-living to spend the hours and days and *years* of your life trying to win the approval of someone who makes it her business to never approve of you? Trying to win the love of someone who can never love? To win the respect of someone who can never respect?

Is that really the best use of your finite time on this planet?

Don't forget that there is a huge opportunity cost to being in touch with her. By this I mean that when you're spending time and energy pandering to her, and recovering from having been hurt by her, this is time and energy in which you are not dancing, or painting, or playing with your children, or hiking or starting a business or whatever else makes your soul sing.

I promise you that the message I hear over and over from DONMs, and one I speak myself is: *My only regret is that I didn't do it years earlier.*

Clearly I have an agenda here, because I do not want to see you waste your life chasing this woman's non-existent approval, and even the fact that I am using words like 'waste' shows my point of view. So do consider the source as you read this. But think too, am I factually wrong?

Regret is a feeling, and, as we said, feelings are messengers from your beliefs, and regret is saying, 'You did the wrong thing'. But as already discussed, these beliefs can be wrong, and I offer you to know that the belief that you have to keep in touch with an abuser is a wrong belief.

I invite you to give yourself permission to live your own best life rather than sacrificing it to an abuser.

Does this all make sense to you? Does it resonate with you? Do you feel the truth of this in your body?

If so, great.

If not, that's understandable. We spoke already of the difference between knowing and KNOWING. To come to a place of KNOWING. I do invite you to play with Tapping, Freewriting and Committee Meetings to resolve this dilemma fully.

9.26: They'll all disapprove of me

You cannot be free from narcissistic abuse and have everyone approve of this decision.

Remember we said that with this narcissistic dynamic, there are often no good options, just your choice of bad options. This is an example of that. The reality is: their good opinion of you or your freedom. Pick one.

And by 'their' I mean anybody – from close family to casual acquaintances – who will have an opinion on you cutting off contact with your narcissistic mother.

Add to that the reality that your mother will no doubt spin your absence in a way that reflects well on her and badly on you. So they are only hearing one side of the story, and it's not your side. Of course they will judge you badly.

It is completely unfair that you have to make this choice between your freedom and their approval. But the good news is that you can free yourself from needing their approval. It's not easy I know. But it is possible, and the result is your freedom.

Be aware that you do run the risk of those others cutting you out of their lives if you go No-Contact. We discussed this earlier but I repeat it now as it is a big consideration. (This is one reason I recommend not going No-Contact until you have finished this resource.)

Don't forget too, that unlike in tribal days, we do have other people we can connect with. We are not limited to one literal tribe. Yes, we might well lose the approval of our mother's circle, but there are eight billion other people in the world for us to connect with.

Now, you might decide that you need their approval more than you need your freedom and peace, more than you need to be treated well, and that is fine. If you do a cost/benefit analysis of it, and this is the decision you make, that is your choice and as such is the right choice for you. This is part of what I meant when I said that this book wasn't about making you go No-Contact, but about creating the freedom to make real choices.

Does this all make sense to you? Does it resonate with you? Do you feel the truth of this in your body?

If so, great.

If not, that's understandable. We spoke already of the difference between knowing and KNOWING. To come to a place of KNOWING. I do invite you to play with Tapping, Freewriting and Committee Meetings to resolve this dilemma fully.

9.27: And then I'll be the bad guy

We just spoke about the overall need for the approval of your mother and her circle, and I include this specific statement too as it is one I hear, word-for-word, from so many DONMs. The implication is that their thinking of you as a bad guy needs to impact on you.

But it's even more than that: I find it interesting that DONMs don't say, *And then they'll call me the bad guy*. Rather, they say, *I'll be the bad guy*. They do mean it in the sense of what others will think, but there is huge acceptance of being the bad guy the way these DONMs phrase it.

Also, I invite you to consider that just because they think you're the bad guy, doesn't mean you are. They have wrong information, both about needing to keep in touch with parents no matter how abusive, in general, and you and your decisions in particular. But you know better.

There is a lot of power to them thinking of you as the

bad guy, because you might well be thinking of yourself as the bad guy too. Many of the Blocking Beliefs we have explored so far are about No-Contact being unfair and nasty to your mother. Hopefully you will now know differently, and I remind you that: it is never wrong to remove yourself from an abuser.

Does this all make sense to you? Does it resonate with you? Do you feel the truth of this in your body?

If so, great.

If not, that's understandable. We spoke already of the difference between knowing and KNOWING. To come to a place of KNOWING. I do invite you to play with Tapping, Freewriting and Committee Meetings to resolve this dilemma fully.

9.28: Your children's grandparents

You need to consider whether – by going No-Contact – you are depriving your children of their grandparents.

I use the word 'deprive' advisedly as that is the word DONMs use when they raise this issue.

But I offer you to consider that instead of depriving your children, you are protecting them.

If your mother is an abuser, she is not safe to have around your children. If she is too toxic for you, as an adult, she is surely too toxic for your children. It is both your right and your duty to protect your children from abusers.

Now, your narcissistic mother might not seem like an abuser to your children, especially if they are young. Narcissists can often behave well with small children, those too young to challenge them yet, or have their own personality or own opinions. So all might be well, or appear well at least, at this stage.

All About Blocking Beliefs

But if she is narcissistic, she is bad news, and if she is kind now, she will not always be kind.

She might also play favourites among your children, making one the Golden Child and one the Scapegoat, and obviously that is a dynamic you do not want for your children.

Another risk to staying in contact with your narcissistic mother is that she might almost literally steal your children: seducing them into preferring her. I have had far too many emails from DONMs whose teenage / adult children are strictly Camp Narcissistic Mother and who are out of touch with their own mothers.

If you decide to go No-Contact, you will have to tell your children (assuming they are old enough to notice), and it can be hard to explain why you are doing this. You can tell them in age-appropriate words that their grandmother is mean, and a bully, and her brain is broken in a way that means she just cannot be nice, so you cannot let her be around you all. Make sure to reassure them that you have to be consistently not-nice, and refuse to become nice, before this happens, in case they think that any minor transgression of theirs would see them cast off too.

DONMs have written to me concerned that this will model to their children that it's okay to cast off relatives, worried that their children will thus cast them off in their turn.

I don't think so.

Instead, this is modelling that we do not allow bullies to keep bullying us, and that's a lesson your children need to learn. And it's modelling that when we cannot fix a relationship, we walk away, and I think that is a valuable lesson for them too.

DONMs who agonise over going No-Contact do so because they were taught that you have to endure bullies if you are related to them, and that is an idea that needs to die.

And you will be creating your own relationship with your children, and they will have no need to abandon you. People don't abandon their parents lightly: look at all the angst and indecision you are experiencing about this decision, after all.

Does this all make sense to you? Does it resonate with you? Do you feel the truth of this in your body?

If so, great.

If not, that's understandable. We spoke already of the difference between knowing and KNOWING. To come to a place of KNOWING. I do invite you to play with Tapping, Freewriting and Committee Meetings to resolve this dilemma fully.

9.29: Guilt revisited

So, now that you have worked through all the Blocking Beliefs, I invite you to check in with your guilt. How does that feel now? Is there any guilt remaining?

If so, it could be because of a blocking belief I haven't covered in this resource. If you are (or become, see below) aware of this blocking belief, I invite you to contact me and tell me it, and I'll investigate this with you to resolve it. I want this resource to be fully comprehensive.

If you are not yet aware of which blocking belief you hold, you can take the following steps:

Feel your guilt but don't believe it
By this I mean that you cannot, in the short term at least, stop the guilt, so you will feel and experience it anyway. However, you don't have to believe it. You don't have to swim in it so to speak. You can calmly observe this guilt feeling from an

emotional distance and think to yourself something like: *Oh, there's that guilt again. It still has the wrong belief that I have to stay in contact with an abuser. But I know it's wrong, so I won't make any decisions based on this feeling.*

Discuss and negotiate with your guilt

Imagine guilt as one of your committee members, and know that it is always trying to help. It just has wrong information. So speak to it as the friend it is. Say things like, 'Guilt, I know that you feel it's wrong to go No-Contact. But I promise you that it's not wrong. It's never wrong to protect myself from an abuser. I'm sure you can agree with that? And my mother is definitely an abuser. So you can relax and let go of this particular issue. Thank you for trying to keep me in integrity, but I promise you that there is nothing to worry about here.'

And then listen to your Guilt and see what it has to say, and go from there.

Freewrite to see what specific issues, if any, you feel guilty about

Write a dialogue with your guilt to investigate further. You write both sides of the discussion, i.e. you, and your guilt as if it is a separate entity.

Use Tapping

There's no script for this as such, as it's just a feeling. Just tap the points in turn, remembering to breathe, as you focus on your feelings of guilt.

10
CHECKING IN: HOW DO YOU FEEL NOW?

At this point in the journey, how do you feel about going No-Contact? Has resolving all those Blocking Beliefs clarified things for you?

If so, great.

And if not, that is no problem at all. The rest of this resource speaks as if you have made the decision to go No-Contact, but if you have not done so yet, don't worry about it, as knowing the process of going No-Contact and the possible fallout of it, and how to manage that fallout, will help you make your decision.

You can go straight onto the next sections, but you might like to journal first, to help you clarify what you're thinking, to check in with yourself in a way.

11
THE PROCESS
OF GOING
NO-CONTACT

11.1: Should you write a No-Contact letter?

You have two options when you decide to go No-Contact: 1) to write her a formal letter, or 2) to just ghost her and let her get the hint.

As ever, what you decide is up to you, but I do strongly suggest that you do write a formal No-Contact letter. This is for your sake as it will give you better closure, and also you can be sure she knows what is going on so if she, say, turns up at your door, you know it's because she is defying No-Contact and not because she is worried about you when she hadn't heard from you, and therefore it will be easier for you to shut the door in her face.

So, what do you write in a No-Contact letter? And just as importantly, what do you *not* write?

What not to write in a No-Contact letter

When you sit down to write your No-Contact letter, it can be extremely tempting to explain to your mother in great detail exactly why you're taking the huge step of severing all contact with her.

There are a number of reasons why you might feel compelled to do this.

The first is the urge to be fair to her. You don't want to be mean or nasty, and so it seems only right that she should understand exactly why you're doing this, rather than it just landing like some sort of bomb.

The second reason is to justify yourself. You know that No-Contact is a huge step, and you need to explain to her why you felt you had no choice but to do it. Maybe she will finally understand all that she has done wrong and will therefore acknowledge – if only to herself – that you had to do this.

The third possible reason is that there is a tiny flicker of hope left, and this hope whispers that if you tell her all that she has done wrong, and show her how bad it is by the fact it has brought you to going No-Contact, then it will give her the reality check she needs and she will change.

Another possible reason is that you want to speak your truth to her in a way you never could before, and this is your last chance.

These reasons are all totally understandable and reasonable, and I suspect most if not all DONMs feel the pull of them. Here's why none of them apply though: They all assume you are dealing with a reasonable person who is capable of understanding more than her own narrow needs.

If your mother is narcissistic, she is not a reasonable person who is capable of understanding anything. You know this. You've done all the discussing and pleading and explaining already, right? And it never worked before. There is zero possibility that it will work this time.

So, in telling her exactly why you're doing this, in a way you are *not* being fair to her. Narcissists experience criticisms as a vicious attack, and your words will wound her. She won't even consider what you have shared about how her actions have hurt you; her only consideration will be how badly your words, your accusations, have hurt her. And even worse: here you are making this vicious attack and not even letting her respond! Or trying not to. If you write what she sees as these nasty horrible untrue attacks she will do all possible to get you to hear her response, to break down your No-Contact wall in other words. And so, writing your truth will only be escalating an already difficult situation.

As for the second reason: to justify yourself to her, to hope that she will finally get it. She won't. No matter how plainly you explain it, in simple words and with citations and examples and illustrations and diagrams, she will not get it. For her fragile ego to remain intact she *needs* to not get it, and she can do not-getting a lot better than you can do explaining. She will never acknowledge that you were right to go No-Contact.

But you know, you can let that be okay, if you decide. You don't need her permission or approval to do this. (Which is just as well as you will never get it.) And so you do not need to explain yourself to her.

As for the third reason: the tiny bit of hope that she might finally change. If this hope is still lurking, I invite you to go back to the section on that, and to work with Freewriting and/or Tapping and/or Committee Members to let it go. This is a hope that traps you and limits you. As we have said already: she cannot change, or she would already have changed, and you have already done all you can to try to create a good and healthy relationship with her.

The poet Emily Dickinson wrote a beautiful poem about hope. The first verse reads:

> 'Hope' is the thing with feathers -
> That perches in the soul -
> And sings the tune without the words -
> And never stops - at all –

The rest of the poem goes on to explore this further: how hope survives despite the strongest storms, and keeps going regardless. The image the poem conjures is of a sweet little bird, plucky despite its small size: a sparrow maybe, or a hummingbird.

And in many ways this concept of hope is appropriate. Hope is essential to us humans to keep us going through a difficult life.

However ...

When it comes to hoping our narcissistic mother will change, I see this bird as a bedraggled vulture perching on our shoulder, ready to fight off any reality that might free us. I think of this vulture feeding on our hopes for freedom, and tearing the flesh off our independence and courage.

In this context, I think hope is a vicious thing that does not serve us.

I do offer you and invite you to let go of this kind of hope if it is still lurking. I invite you to turn your hope to your own life and your own future and your freedom from abuse. I invite you to hope for your independence and healing. And to claim those things too, which is what No-Contact will do for you. There is an EFT / Tapping Script available via donm.info/ htgnc-resources to help you let go of that useless hope if you would like to check that out.

As for the fourth reason: you can absolutely speak your truth, and we will do that. Just not to her. It will serve no purpose to speak your truth to her: she is completely unable to hear it, and it will feel like an attack to her, and you will be inviting some kind of backlash. The best way to go No-Contact is to invite as little drama as possible, and speaking your truth to her is the opposite of that.

Write your truth for yourself

So, no, do not write your truth in the No-Contact letter you will send her. By all means write this letter for yourself. Speaking our truth is essential, even if she will never hear it.

I offer you to write a No-Holds-Barred No-Contact letter. In this letter pour out all you want to say to her: all the hurt and anger and unfairness. All the examples of her meanness and nastiness. All the missed chances for kindness.

Knowing that she will not read it means that you do not have to censor yourself or try to be kind, or offer excuses for her.

Write your truth, write it all down, as bad and bald as it was.

And then keep this letter safely along with your *Greatest Hits*, to read if you start second-guessing yourself in the future.

Now, this letter might well be upsetting to write, so don't feel you have to do it either. It is totally up to you. You might choose not to write it at all, or to write it in manageable stages. Also, don't forget that if you do get upset, you can always use Tapping to process that upset and move it on in a healthy way: just tap all the points in turn as you are experiencing the pain. You don't even have to say anything. Just tap, and breathe. And consciously try to breathe from your diaphragm, i.e. deep breaths, rather than from just your chest/throat, i.e. shallow breaths. The automatic reaction when we're upset is shallow breaths, but consciously remembering to breathe deeply will help calm you too.

11.2: What to write in a No-Contact letter

The trick is to keep it short and sweet. Tell her enough so that you have closure, and you know she knows, but without detail.

Here is an example, very closely based on what I wrote myself:

Mum, it is with regret that I realise our relationship is not healthy, and cannot ever be healthy. Therefore I will not contact you again. I ask you not to contact me either, and if you do, I will not read or listen to it, nor respond.

[Your name]

So, now I invite you to write your No-Contact letter, bearing in mind all that we have discussed, and your own decisions, and then, when you are ready, to send it to her. I do recommend that you send it recorded post/mail so that you can be certain she got it and can evaluate any of her future actions on that basis, rather than second-guessing the situation.

If you would like to use this text, I share it on donm. info/htgnc-resources in a form that you can just copy and paste.

If you are not ready to send your letter yet, that's perfectly fine: just continue with the rest of the book to see what might happen if you do, because we next discuss what might happen after she receives your No-Contact letter and how to deal with it all.

11.3: Temporary No-Contact

I am hoping that since you have worked through this resource so far, and we have hopefully knocked down all the blocks to No-Contact, that you won't be conflicted about it now.

But just in case, I offer you the option of time-limited No-Contact. This can be a good option if you are not ready to burn all the bridges right now, but you definitely need a break from her. It can give you a test-run period of No-Contact to see how you feel without her in your life. If this works for you, at the end of the designated period of time, you can write to her and tell her that No-Contact is now permanent, if that is what you decide.

Be aware though that if you do go back to her after a period of No-Contact like this, she will almost certainly punish you with extra nastiness. She might not do it immediately as there might be a honeymoon period first where she is extra nice. But she will do the nastiness at some stage. She will have to punish you for daring to reject her at all, plus there is all the pent-up nastiness that she didn't get to dump on you during your break from her. (But of course, you can then go No-Contact again, permanently this time, if that is what you choose.)

Or, she may refuse to accept you back. You need to be aware of this possibility. Whether she accepts you back or not will depend on how much Narcissistic Supply she is getting from others, how much drama your absence is feeding her versus how much drama your return will give her and so on. So it's impossible to predict whether she'll do that.

One thing I can predict with certainty though is that if you do go back, there will be zero talk about what happened, and no discussions, no resolutions, nothing. You'll both be pretending that your absence never happened.

If you decide on a time-limited No-Contact period you could write something like:

Mom, I have been struggling with our relationship this last while, and I need some time away from it. I am not going to be in contact until [date], and I ask you to respect this and not contact me either. If you do, I will ignore it.

[Your name]

If you would like to use this text, I share it on donm.info/htgnc-resources in a form that you can just copy and paste.

11.4: Conditional No-Contact

You might want to leave the door open for re-establishing contact with your mother if she takes responsibility for what she is doing and genuinely changes.

As an interesting aside, I was working with a DONM coaching client to guide her through speaking with her committee members, and it was one of her committee members who came up with this possibility. That committee member felt they would be comfortable going No-Contact if they gave the narcissistic mother the option of redemption.

Now, it's important to know that I include this in order to give you comprehensive options rather than steering you in any specific direction, but please don't take this as my recommendation to actually do this. If your mother is narcissistic she is incapable of owning her flaws or genuinely changing. You will be doing this so that you know you have been completely fair to her. And if you don't want to offer her this option, that is completely fair too: I remind you that you have tried over and over to resolve things with her. She's already had more than enough last chances. You can use the following text:

> *Mum, it is with regret that I realise our relationship is not healthy, and I do not see how it can ever become healthy. Therefore I will not contact you again. I ask you not to contact me either unless you are willing to own and acknowledge all that you have done wrong to me, and prove your willingness to treat me better going forward. If you want to do this, [contact me] with your thoughts on how you will do that. Do not text or phone me, and if you do I will not answer or respond.*
>
> *[Your name]*

If you would like to use this text, I share it on donm.info/ htgnc-resources in a form that you can just copy and paste.

I strongly suggest you set up a specific way for her to contact you. Either your existing email address, or a new one you create specifically. Or, another option is to ask her to email a partner or friend who is both trustworthy and knowledgeable about NPD: they can read it and tell you if she is serious or just messing. Or ask her to post/mail you a letter. This option means she will have to go to a bit of trouble to contact you and should cut out any spur-of-the-moment self-pity parties she's sharing with you.

For sure though, do (I suggest) as the above text says, and tell her not to phone or text you. Doing this will keep those avenues of communication safe for you from the stress of hearing from her.

11.5: Build your No-Contact Wall

When you decide to go No-Contact, your most important job is to build a virtual wall that she cannot breach to get access to you. This wall serves two purposes:

- It blocks her from your life so that you and she are not in contact in any way. This is the essence of No-Contact.
- It keeps you safe from her. With this wall in place, she can sob and play victim and have her narcissistic rages all she wants – *but you will not know about it!* That's the essential bit.

To build this No-Contact Wall you make the decision that you will:
- Never ever ever speak to her again (unless you choose to break No-Contact, of which more below).

- Block her on social media, and make sure you don't follow her either.
- Not speak to her, no matter what is going on, or what tricks she tries. (We'll speak more of her tricks shortly.)
- Not listen to her, no matter what is going on or what tricks she tries.
- Have no direct communication with her. Necessary communication only through solicitors or lawyers.
- Not send her invitations to anything or accept any of her invitations.
- Not answer the phone to her.
- Not listen to her voicemails.
- Block her number.
- Not read or answer emails. Save her emails in case you need to take legal action. (We discuss later why you might want or need to do that.)
- Not send any cards or gifts, no matter the occasion.
- Not open any cards or 'gifts' that she sends you.
- Decline to discuss her with others.
- If practical, ask others not to discuss you with her.
- Not go to see her on her death bed, or attend her funeral.

Each of these is a brick in your No-Contact wall, and they are all essential in order not to leave gaps.

The above is nothing less than your No-Contact Manifesto, and I invite you to either hand write it out (for the 'ownership' of that) or print it out. On the top put 'I will ...' and sign it at the bottom.

Block her on social media

The ideal after No-Contact is that your mother doesn't have any access to your life, and curating your social media is a very important part of that.

I invite you to visit the resources page on donm.info/htgnc-resources to access information on how to block your narcissistic mother on all the main social media platforms.

One problem however is that she can set up new accounts and follow you that way.

Depending on the social media itself, there are ways to lock down your content, but often that defeats the whole purpose of having social media in the first place. You might use it professionally for example and so you can't lock it down too much.

However, you can certainly stop her from contacting you directly, and that has huge value by itself.

And you can decide that if you can't control what she sees about your life, then there's no point worrying about it. There might even be some satisfaction in knowing that she is watching you live your best life from her bitter, silenced, pathetic life.

But also you might want to curate what you share based on the possibility, probability, or even fact that she will access it. Yes this is frustrating and annoying, but it's also part of the reality of this narcissistic dynamic.

I invite you to visit the resources page on donm.info/htgnc-resources where I share information on how to block your narcissistic mother on all the main social media platforms.

12
POSSIBLE FALLOUT

Once you send the No-Contact letter, what might happen next?

You may well be very nervous, like waiting for an axe to fall. Don't forget that you have the option of Tapping to help you through this stressful time. And hopefully you have built your wall so she should not be able to reach you.

We will discuss the various steps she might take. Bear in mind that if you have built your No-Contact wall, you won't be even aware of any of these and she'll be shouting into the void. But we will deal with these attempts as if she has managed to get through that wall, and give you suggestions to help you deal with them.

12.1: There might be no reaction

There's a possibility that nothing will happen at all, that your mother will not react in any way. We'll never know, but maybe she just shrugged and got on with her life.

If this is the case, it can really, really hurt. To know that you had tried and tried so hard all these years to create a relationship with her, and she just didn't care enough even to try to contact you?

Or maybe did care, and was upset, but took you at your word and didn't get in touch. This can hurt too, even though it is what we asked for. To think that she could walk away so easily, without even trying to fix things: that is so painful.

The reality though is that this is no new information. You already knew that she didn't love you or care for you. You have had ample proof of that your whole life. This is just one more proof.

But yes, it hurts, and that's normal and reasonable. In a way it's her last – and possibly worst – rejection.

Just know that ignoring your instructions and contacting you doesn't mean she values you more than if she just accepts your No-Contact letter. It just means that she doesn't want to lose her chew toy.

So, logically, her not contacting you again is no worse than her insisting on contacting you again.

Either of these actions is the same: the manifestation of her narcissism. The only difference is in her head: whether she thinks it will serve her needs better to just abandon you and concentrate on her other sources of narcissistic supply (and possibly get lots more supply by playing up the drama of you abandoning her), or her pursuing you and trying to reel you back.

Neither of those options is about her realising how serious things are and trying to fix things.

But I understand entirely that logic doesn't come into it when you are – as we all are – this hurt little girl crying for her mother, and the pain of this rejection. I know it. I experienced it.

So I am definitely not trying to argue you out of this pain. These words are just to help you somewhat when you are the other side of the pain.

For now, you need to help to process the pain. I have created an EFT/Tapping script to help with the pain of this: *Erase The Hurt She Dropped You So Easily,* and it's available via the Resources page. I invite you to use that, or your own Tapping words, to help ease this pain.

And, no matter how much it hurts, I promise you that this outcome is truly the best and easiest. If she contacts you in any way, that brings its own complexities, and we discuss those next.

Also, be aware that even if your mother doesn't contact you immediately, she might do so after a period of time. My own mother did exactly this. Now, the situation was slightly different because No-Contact was initiated after a last, fraught, phone conversation which ended with us both hanging up, after which neither of us initiated contact in any way for nine full months. For my side, I was just enjoying the peace, and I have no idea what she was thinking. But nine months later was my birthday, and she sent me an innocuous birthday card, along with a bought cheesy little poem that purported to say sorry 'for whatever I've done' but also said I shouldn't be bearing grudges. And it was upon receipt of those contact-bombs that I wrote my No-Contact letter.

So even if there is silence at first, I do suggest you familiarise yourself with the rest of the information in this resource, just in case she does contact you in the future.

12.2: She might initiate a welfare check

The narcissistic mothers need to spin a narrative about why you've gone No-Contact that absolves them of any liability, responsibility, culpability or guilt.

And so sometimes they create the narrative that you have been hurt, or under the sway of an abusive partner who's isolating you from your loving family, or are having a psychotic episode. All of that is still – in their reality-lite – more plausible than them being in any way wrong.

So, they have been known to contact their daughter's

local police station asking them to do a welfare check, and the police duly turn up at your door.

This one is very easy to solve: just tell the police you're fine and once they see you and hear that all is good they will go away happy.

Or, you could even contact the police pre-emptively and tell them that you are about to cut off contact with your mother and they might hear from her but they have no need to worry as you are fine.

So, this possible reaction is very low-stakes, but it has been known to happen so I wanted you to be aware of the possibility.

12.3: She might turn up at your door

Another decision you need to make is what you will do in the event that she just turns up at your door. You are best served by planning for this so if it does happen, you are in a position to handle it.

Decide ahead of time what you will do, rather than trying to make a decision in the moment when you will be under stress.

You may decide that you simply will not answer the door (if you realise ahead of time that it's her). That is the simplest option. Maybe go to an inside room: your bedroom maybe, where you can't hear her knocking, or at least you feel some distance from her. If you do decide this, I strongly suggest that you let her knock for as long as she wants without giving in to her. It's the only way she'll learn that you mean what you say. If you give in to her after say half an hour of knocking, she'll just learn that that's what it takes to provoke a reaction from you. So, hard as it is, just leave her to it. Maybe put on headphones so you can't hear her, and/or read a book, and/or tap if you're finding it stressful.

Definitely note when she came and how long she stayed, in case you need to file a restraining order at some stage. (I include a tracking form in the Printables via donm.info/htgnc-resources.) It might seem cowardly to just hide, but this is tactical hiding: sometimes the most powerful thing we can do is to do nothing.

You can always call the police on her for trespass and harassment, but obviously that is a big decision and not to be taken lightly.

If you do answer the door to her without realising it's her, then know that you have zero obligation to talk to her. You can calmly but firmly close the door.

It might feel wrong to even consider closing the door in her face. That is beyond mere rudeness, isn't it? But again, we're allowed to be what others call rude, what our conditioning and Society's beliefs tell us is rude, but is really only boundaries.

I would instead say that she is the one who is being beyond mere rudeness. You have told her not to contact you (if you did send a No-Contact letter and this situation is exactly why I recommend doing that) and she is ignoring this to such an extent that she is invading your space. Talk about ignoring your boundaries. Talk about being rude!

In a way this situation is a microcosm of all we have been discussing in this book: that you can do what is right for you, once it's moral and ethical, despite Society's so-called rules saying otherwise. It reminds us that we don't have to be in any situation that we don't want to be in.

Nothing obliges you to be in a conversation or situation

you don't choose. Don't let Society's stories and your mother's wishes tell you differently. You are the boss of you.

And, to be in a position to close the door in her face when needed, do rehearse that. Literally physically open a door, imagine you see her the other side of it, and close it again. You might choose to say briefly, 'No,' as you close it, to train your body how that is different from normal general door-closing. Probably you'd be better off to practise by using an internal door rather than your front door, because that might look very odd to the neighbours. Your body will learn what it needs to, even using an internal door.

Now, what if you decide that if your mother turns up at your door, that you *will* listen to what she has to say?

First of all I remind you that you already tried everything you could and it never worked.

Secondly, I remind you that by turning up like this she is *proving* that she hasn't changed, because she is completely willing to ignore your wishes and boundaries (assuming you sent a No-Contact letter that stated your wishes and boundaries).

But if you wish to hear her out even so, that is completely your choice. You are the boss of you.

It's hard to give advice for how this should go, as there are so many variables. But here are some thoughts, and I invite you to decide ahead of time how you will respond based on the following ideas. If you decide ahead of time, then you won't have to create your response in the moment when you are under stress.

First: don't invite her in. Ideally talk to her on the doorstep or a neutral venue. If she gets into your house, you're stuck with her there and it would be difficult and messy to stop the conversation when you want to.

Now, if she won't accept this and insists on coming in, that is really good information for you that she has not changed, that she's still trying to have it all her own way, and that she can't want to talk to you that badly if she's putting conditions on it. You need only say firmly, 'Here or not at all, choose one.' And if she keeps insisting, then definitely (I suggest) just calmly close the door. She had her chance and she blew it.

Second: do more listening than talking. Let her say what she's going to say.

Third: if she's asking you questions, answer them as minimally as you can, if at all. You are in an information-gathering process, rather than being obliged to explain yourself. There is an acronym: *JADE*, which stands for *Justify, Argue, Defend, Explain*, and the trick with narcissists is that you don't do any of those things. You don't *justify* your No-Contact decision to her. You don't *argue* with her: that never ends well with a narcissist, and you're not trying to win her over to any point of view right now; you're past that point. You don't *defend* yourself: again, no need to get her to see your point of view, and she won't anyway. And you don't *explain* yourself, because she won't be able to hear it.

Fourth: Once she has said what she needs to say, rather than you feeling obliged to respond to her in the moment, I invite you to give yourself permission to tell her that you'll think about what she said and get back to her if that's what you decide. This is to give you time to think calmly about what she has said rather than feeling under pressure in the moment.

This is another situation in which her reaction will give you really good information. If she insists on you making any commitment or concession in the moment, that is definite proof that she hasn't changed no matter what she has just said. You can say, 'If you insist on an answer now, the answer is no.'

Indeed, I further suggest that you practise saying, 'I'll

think about what you said and get back to you,' so that the phrase comes naturally to you.

Fifth: you can end the conversation at any time by simply saying, 'This conversation is over,' and closing the door. Or just closing the door without saying anything. This especially applies if she starts verbally abusing you. Again, I suggest you practise this skill. And yes, this might feel rude, but it is not. It is boundaries, and you are allowed to have those.

Exercise 15: Decide what you will do if she comes to the door. You can call a Committee Meeting on this, or Freewrite, or Tap if you struggle to know the best thing to do. Decide:

- Whether you will answer the door to her or not, and if you do,
- Where you will engage with her, e.g. your doorstep, or a nearby café.

Exercise 16: Practise the following actions and phrases until they become comfortable and automatic:

- Closing the door in her face. You can practise with an internal door. Just picture her there, and then physically close the door so your body gets used to that.
- 'You can't come in but I am willing to talk to you here.' (Or wherever you decide of course.)
- 'I have nothing to say to you, but I am willing to listen to you.'

- 'Thank you for sharing your thoughts with me. I will consider what you have said and will get back to you if I decide there is merit in doing that.'
- 'This conversation is over, goodbye.' And then you close the door.

I have a role-play video available via the resources section to help you practise this skill, if you think this would help.

12.4: Stop this nonsense!

One thing your mother might say to you, at the door or elsewhere, is a demand that you stop this nonsense now. Or other words to say the same thing: 'This has gone on long enough!' or 'You need to get over yourself!'

There is an infinity of phrases she can use, but the message is the same in each case: she is insisting that you go back to the way things were. All without her acknowledging any wrong-doing or making any effort to change, of course.

This can be hard to resist, because all your life you were used to doing exactly what she told you.

But you don't need to play her game any longer. Just because she says it, doesn't mean you have to. You are the boss of you.

If she does say this, it is proof that she has not changed one bit, and that is all the confirmation you need that she has not changed, and you can completely ignore this.

12.5: She tries to harm you

Narcissists *hate* rejection. For sure, none of us like to be rejected, but narcissists *hate* it. How can anybody possibly reject their perfection, after all? Rejection says to them that they're not the wonderful person they must believe themselves to be, and this is a complete attack on their world-view, and they react accordingly. There is no fury like a narcissist scorned.

So your narcissistic mother might well try to take her revenge on you for this rejection in whatever way she can. This is why we already spoke of not going No-Contact if she has any power over you such as a job or housing situation.

But even if you think she doesn't have much power over you, she might try to do as much damage as she can by contacting people who have, or could have, power over you. This can apply even if she doesn't know these people personally.

One favourite trick – I have heard of this from far too many DONMs – is to try to get you into trouble with Child Protection Services by reporting you to them for neglecting your children. Luckily this shouldn't come to anything as the investigation will clear you as it'll be obvious all is well. But the stress of going through this cannot be underestimated. I can't think of any way of pre-empting this to prevent it happening, but at least be emotionally prepared for it.

Another thing they can try is to contact your employer to tell them how awful you are and to try to get you fired. Yes, this is unhinged. But again: no fury like a narcissist scorned. You can pre-empt this by warning your employer and any similar contacts, if this is appropriate for you, and suggest they don't even take the call from her.

You can use the following text, if you like:

'Dear X, I am writing to advise you of something that might happen in the near future. I have realised that my mother [name] is toxic and abusive, and I have cut off contact with her for my own safety. As part of this toxicity she may well contact you to lie to you to try to cause me difficulties. You have known me for X years, and you know I am a good and ethical person based on your experiences with me such as [list some examples if you like], and I ask you to consider all of this if you choose to listen to her. I am sorry to bring you into this situation, and would not do so if I could trust my mother to act in a reasonable way. If you have any questions I am happy to answer them. Regards [You]

Obviously only add the bit about being happy to answer questions if you are comfortable with that. Also, note that I include this text at donm.info/htgnc-resources so you can copy and paste it easily.

> Exercise 17: Write a list of places, people and organisations that your mother has access to, and work out a strategy towards pre-empting any attempted attack on you.

One thing your Narcissistic Mother will almost definitely do is to launch a smear campaign against you even with people who don't have power over you but who you value, and we discuss this next.

12.6: Smear campaigns

One way narcissists react to you going No-Contact is to create smear campaigns, i.e. to complain about you at length to everyone they can force to listen: their own circle, your extended family, your community, your church, and so on.

They may admit you have gone No-Contact and use that to complain about your ingratitude and your nastiness and how they never did anything wrong to you and in fact were a wonderful mother but nothing ever pleased you anyway so what could anyone expect.

Or she might make up complete and utter lies about you and say she had to cut you off because of whatever she says you did.

Needless to say her list of complaints will bear little or no resemblance to reality.

There is very little that can be done to protect yourself from smear campaigns as people seem to believe what they hear, and won't ask you for your side of it. You most likely will not even know what she is saying about you, and will have no chance to defend yourself. But you'll find people treat you differently, distance themselves from you maybe. This is yet another way the narcissistic abuse is so damaging.

You can try to speak to your extended family but don't forget that your mother has already created dynamics that suit her, and that the family members are tied to her by a variety of fear, hope for inheritance, belief in her, etc.

As for other people such as those in your local community or church or similar, it's very possible that they adore your mother. These narcissists are excellent at projecting a good image of themselves. And so of course they're going to believe her.

You can of course contact these people pre-emptively as

I suggested in the previous section, and using the same text if that works for you. The problem with this is that these people do know her already, and she has had years of spinning her stories and agendas. It's a tough decision, and only you can decide if it's worth it.

Because of these Smear Campaigns, one of the sad realities of going No-Contact is that you risk losing these people from your life too. Some you won't mind about; others will be a huge loss. Remember our motto: there are no good options when it comes to the narcissistic dynamic, but only your choice of bad options. The only way to win back the good opinion of these people is to resign yourself to forever putting up with your Narcissistic Mother's abuse. Is the opinion of these people worth that? Only you can decide that.

And of course it is going to hurt if you lose them. Remember what we shared about Maslow's Hierarchy of Needs, and the Need To Belong. These people are, to a greater or lesser extent, your tribe, and you need to belong to them and instead they are shunning you. This is not easy at all and is part of the price of your freedom.

If you decide that your freedom from abuse is worth more than these people's opinion of you, try to concentrate on communities that she doesn't have access to, and create your post-narcissistic life where she cannot intrude. Yes, this is huge upheaval and yes it's completely unfair. But it's the way it is, unfortunately. Remember that we said that this narcissistic dynamic leaves you with no good options, but only your choice of bad options, and this is a perfect example of that.

Don't forget that you can use Tapping, Freewriting and Committee Members to help you erase the stress around Smear Campaigns. These resources cannot change the reality, but they can help you have peace about it.

12.7: She tries to win you back

If your Narcissistic Mother doesn't try to harm you or to turn people against you – or, even, at the same time as she's doing those things, or once she's tried those and they fail – she might try to win you back.

She might do this regardless of whether you left the door open with a conditional No-Contact letter, or not.

I remind you that if she does this, it does not mean she loves, values and respects you. It means she wants her chew toy back. I am sorry to be blunt, but this is the reality. She had literally your whole life to show you love, value, and respect, and she did not.

She has a variety of tactics she can try, and it can be very tempting to fall for some of these. After all, all you wanted your whole life was your mother's love and esteem, and here it is looking as if you are going to get those. That is hard to resist. If you do fall for these tricks, that's okay too, and we'll discuss that later.

As we discuss the various tricks she might try, bear in mind that if your No-Contact wall is strong enough, you won't even know about them. But just in case your mother breaches the wall, we need to discuss these tricks.

12.7.1: She plays victim

Nobody is better at throwing themselves a pity-party than narcissists, and your mother will feel very sorry for herself at your No-Contact decision. This self-pity can be at the same time as anger, or after it, or in whatever order it suits her narrative.

She was a wonderful mother; she did everything for you,

and here you are abandoning her for no reason, and that's so unfair to her and she doesn't deserve it and she feels so sad bwaahhhhhhh.

You may be sure this narrative will form part of her smear campaigns as she looks for sympathy from others.

But it can also form part of the way she appeals to you.

She can turn up at your door/outside your place-of-work/outside church or wherever she knows she can find you, sobbing – perhaps literally, but certainly metaphorically – about how hurt she is, how much she misses you, how could you do this to her, etc?

This can be so difficult to resist. It pushes very tender buttons.

The first button is guilt

All our lives we were taught that we had to meet our mother's needs and that belief is deeply ingrained. And here we are ignoring her needs, and she is suffering, and we have the power to stop that suffering. This is deep stuff and very hard to resist.

I remind you that feelings/emotions such as guilt are messengers from our beliefs, and that our beliefs are not always accurate. And as DONMs, our beliefs about what we owe our mothers are especially inaccurate.

The feelings of guilt will come automatically, as they are wired in for now, but we don't have to believe those feelings, and we certainly don't have to act upon them.

Guilt is for when we do something wrong, and removing ourselves from an abuser is never wrong.

The second button is pity

Certainly a sad and weeping narcissist is a pity-inducing figure. They're good at that. (And if I sound cynical, that's because I am.) She wants to make you pity her, so that you will stop doing the thing that hurts her – i.e. removing yourself.

And you know, she genuinely is hurting. I have no doubt of that. She is losing something she values. Not you as a person, but rather the source of attention and drama and whipping-boy that you represent. As I said earlier, she doesn't want to lose her chew toy.

So it wouldn't be a bit surprising that you feel a surge of pity for her too. You don't want to hurt anyone – and I know this from the very fact you are reading this book rather than just shrugging and walking away from her – and here she is hurting badly.

As ever, you are the boss of you, and obviously do whatever you choose in this case. I do invite you though to make decisions that are for your highest good, and based on true information and not false beliefs.

A narcissist's pity is only ever for themselves and their loss.

So, we can accept that your narcissistic mother is genuinely upset, and also acknowledge that this is about her narcissism and self-pity, and not about her being willing to work things out so she has a healthy relationship with you.

And by all means pity her, and all credit to you for that, but you can pity her from a safe distance, and not let that pity influence your actions.

The third button is your hope

We spoke before of how hope can trap us, and if our mother is so upset at our departure this can trigger our hope. Surely she wouldn't be this upset if she didn't value us and want us! It makes perfect sense. All we have wanted, all our lives, is for her to love us and value us, and here she is – it seems – expressing her desire for our company. Hope can spring up, teasing us and tempting us. It's seductive.

I urge you to resist this seduction though. Your mother being upset at losing you is about nothing but the loss of her own wishes and desires. If your cat brings a mouse into the house and you take the mouse away from it, the cat will be truly upset at the loss, and will miaow piteously and look everywhere for the mouse. The cat genuinely misses the mouse, but as prey, not as a friend with whom to create a mutually loving and respectful relationship. Again I remind you of the Tapping Script available via the Resources page about how to let go of this hope.

The fourth button is your urge to fix things for her, as you have been trained to do all your life

This is not your problem to fix. The only solution that she will accept is for you to come back into her life on her terms, and continue to let her abuse you, and that is no solution at all. You do not have to sacrifice your whole Self to her selfishness.

I do offer, via the Resources page, Tapping Scripts to help you release these beliefs. Or use Tapping using your own words, and/or a Committee Meeting to resolve this.

Or grit your teeth and fist your hands and refuse to give in to this urge to fix things for her.

12.7.2: She 'apologises'

As part of the attempt to win you back, your mother might apologise. But it won't be a real apology; it will only be a *fauxpology*.

A fauxpology is, as the word suggest, a false apology. It's a statement which masquerades as an apology when it is no such thing.

Fauxpologies are a favourite trick of narcissists and other abusers.

Here are some examples. See if you can figure out what's wrong with them before you read my explanation, if you like.

I'm sorry you're upset

In this example they are sorry that something has happened, for sure. They are sorry for the circumstances of the person they are speaking to. They are saying sorry in the same way we say to a bereaved person, 'I'm sorry for your loss.' This does not mean we are taking responsibility for the bereavement, obviously.

And this is the meaning of *I'm sorry* that narcissistic mothers are using in this context.

They are not acknowledging anything wrong they did themselves. The issue is your upset, not their actions.

I'm sorry you think I wasn't a good mother

Again, they're sorry for a situation rather than any of their own actions, but this one is even worse because what they're saying sorry for is your thoughts and opinions. How dare they apologise for those! And the implication of course is that your opinion (about her mothering qualities in this example) is wrong. So what she's really saying is that she's sorry you're misguided.

I'm sorry you can't take a joke

Here she is also disappointed, this time because you didn't find whatever she did to be as amusing as she did. So the problem is your lack of sense of humour, and not her actions.

I'm sorry for any offence I might have cause

This is a double-layered fauxpology. She is sorry for any offence. But offence is something you feel, not something she did. So she's still not acknowledging what she did. And even then the offense is only something that *might* have happened. She's in denial about that too!

I'm sorry about ...
Sometimes instead of saying *I'm sorry for*, they will distance themselves even further from it and say, *I'm sorry about ...* This implies that it is an incident completely independent of them, the way you'd say *I'm sorry about your car accident.*

I'm sorry so many bad things happened between us
Holy Passive Voice, Batman! Bad things just happened. And they were between us, not from her to you.

I hope that now that these fauxpologies have been deconstructed, that you can see how they only sound like apologies. In contrast, here is the anatomy of a real apology:

> I did X. That was wrong. I am sorry. To make up I will do Y. Going forward I will make sure I don't do X again by doing Z.

A real apology fully and honestly acknowledges what the person did. They own it fully without excuse. They admit that it was wrong to do (or this can be implied). They arrange to make amends. They tell you what steps they are taking to avoid the same mistake again.

So, for example:

> I forgot your birthday. I am so sorry. I'll bring you out to dinner this weekend instead. And I'll be sure to put it in my calendar so I never forget again.

One clue is to look for the word *but*. If people use the word *but*, anything before the *but* can be discarded as it's not what they mean; what they're really saying is after the *but*.

So here's an example of that:

I'm sorry for forgetting your birthday, but I was really busy.

Do you see how them bringing in the excuse of them being busy totally overrides their apology? The *but* implies they couldn't do anything else than forget your birthday because they were so busy. So this example is not a genuine apology.

Now, if they give the excuse before the but, and the apology afterwards, the excuse becomes an explanation but they are not letting themselves off the hook for it. Like this:

I'm so sorry I forgot your birthday. I've been so busy, but I should have remembered it even so.

Do you see the difference?

One trick the narcissists can try is to offer a blanket apology, such as:

I apologise for all I did wrong.

This one can be very confusing. There's no *but* there, and she is owning what she did, right?

Wrong.

First, it actually is not admitting any bad behaviour. Their loophole is that apologising for all you did wrong doesn't apply if you didn't do anything wrong! That's just science.

And secondly, this apology is so vague as to be useless.

It doesn't acknowledge any specific bad behaviour, nor makes any amends, nor promises any changes, nor offers any specifics of how she will do better in future.

If you want to call your mother's bluff on this one, you can always say something like:

'I appreciate that. I do need you though to give me some examples of the things you did wrong and how you'll avoid them going forward, and things you think you did right so we can discuss those if needed.'

And watch her explode:

'I apologised! What more do you want? Flesh?! Are you trying to humiliate me?'

If she is asked to be specific, she will not be able to be, and that will give you all the information you need.

12.7.3: Love-Bombing

Love-bombing is a phrase borrowed from what cults do when they are trying to seduce you into their ranks.

It means pretty much what it says: to overwhelm you with love. Actually, of course it's not love at all. Instead they seek to overwhelm you with kindness, and attention, and compliments, etc. in order that you *feel* that you are loved. And then, when you are hooked on the good feeling that that brings, they deprive you of it abruptly so that you will do what it takes to get it back.

Abusers do exactly the same. When it comes to narcissists trying to get new prey, we call it the idealisation-devaluation phases. They first idealise you: you are perfect, and wonderful, and exactly who they were waiting for their whole life. And once you are hooked, they will devalue you.[4]

We never had the idealisation stage with our mothers as we were born into captivity so to speak, but if we pull away and go No-Contact she may try this trick of idealising you.

She may sob that she loves you, and misses you, and is so sorry that you feel she didn't love you, and is so sorry you felt you had to pull away. I'm sure you can see the fauxpologies tucked into this.

She may send gifts to you, and cards or letters full of protestations of her love for you and how she wants to try again and if only you'll forgive her. And of course, such forgiveness is to come without any promises or attempts on her behalf to change her behaviour going forward.

Even knowing of this tactic ahead of time, it can be an extremely difficult one to protect yourself from. All your life all you have wanted is her love and attention and care, and here she is heaping it onto you, pouring it out abundantly. It feels so damn good. Of course it does: that is not a character flaw in you; that is just human nature.

Just know that if you do fall for this tactic, and go back to her, that this love-bombing will not last. This is not a real change of heart for her; this is a tactic for her to get what she wants. And it costs her hugely to do this. She is going completely against her nature and her desires to do this. Have you ever held magnets so that the North-North sides are touching? If so, you know how much effort it takes to overcome what the magnets 'want' to do, and the minute you relax, they turn to their natural North-South orientation.

Yep, exactly that.

---

[4] As an aside, this is a good reason to be wary of anyone who falls for you too quickly, or seems to, or who puts you on a pedestal or seems to.

Not only is it that she cannot keep it up, but that she doesn't even see why she should try. Once this love-bombing achieved its aim, why would she want to keep doing it?

And it's worse than that: Once the honeymoon period is over, no doubt there will be a period of her being extra nasty to you, even beyond the normal levels of nastiness that had you going No-Contact.

This can be for a combination of two reasons. The first is that she has all the pent-up nastiness to get out of her system, and the second is that she needs to punish you for daring to leave her and for forcing her to be nice to you even temporarily.

Having said all this, it is totally your decision if you wish to go back to her on this basis. Either she will continue to be kind and loving to you, in which case, yay! Maybe she wasn't narcissistic at all and you can have a good relationship. Or she will turn on you as explained above, in which case, you have this information and can go No-Contact again.

Many DONMs take several attempts to completely go No-Contact, and that's completely okay, and it would be for you too. This is a huge step with so many implications and permutations, that it's not surprising that we feel the need to try to have a relationship with our mother again.

The cost for refusing to fall for her love-bombing is endless wondering, and the cost for trying again is rejection and hurt. As ever with the narcissistic dynamic, there are no good options, only your choice from a selection of bad options.

12.7.4: She sends cards and 'gifts'

I put 'gifts' in inverted commas (quotes) because they are not genuine gifts at all; rather they are a form of manipulation. They are bait.

She knows that the social contract requires you to thank the giver for gifts and even for cards, and so she is using this to force you to contact her.

You are under zero obligation to do this! You're not anyway, but especially not when it's all such manipulation. If your mother was serious about fixing things with you she would be saying, 'What went wrong, and how can I fix it?' Or, given that you've probably told her many times what was wrong: 'I hear what you said, and here's what I'm doing to fix it.'

Sending these bait-gifts is not making any serious effort to fix the relationship, and as such, requires no response from you.

Ideally, don't even open the card or the gift. You don't want to know what she is saying to you. If it's all nice and gushy, then it's manipulation, and there may well be digs and nastiness in there too.

My own mother, after nine months of No-Contact, sent me a birthday card, and I did open it as I did not know then what I know now.

The printed greeting in the birthday card was fine: nice, pleasant, banal. And my mother just signed it with her and my father's name, if memory serves. There was certainly nothing nasty in it, nor anything effusive.

However, enclosed with the card was a shop-bought credit-card sized laminated cheesy rhyme. I wish I'd kept it so that I could quote it exactly, but alas I did not. I do know that it was basically a generic *Sorry–for–whatever–I–did*. The apology had to be non-specific as this was mass-produced, and I half-laughed-half-cried at how she wasn't willing to give a personal and informed apology but rather she expected this cheesy generic dross to make everything okay.

And more: after the apology the poem went into some detail about how it wasn't right to bear grudges and how we should forgive.

And there it was. The zing. The dig. The implied criticism. The *get–over–it* message.

Remember I said earlier that if you get someone else to read the communication, that they should know about Narcissistic Personality Disorder so they aren't fooled by the surface message? This is a classic example of that. On the surface it all seems nice and wanting-to-fix-things: the card, the apology. But when you know how narcissists operate, that's when you see that the apology was generic and owned no bad behaviour and had no promises to change within it, and that it was dumping the responsibility for the estrangement back onto me by saying I was bearing a grudge.

Likewise a gift from your mother probably isn't worth opening. I bet that your mother, like all narcissists, was always really bad at buying presents anyway. To be a good present-buyer, the person needs to a) care enough about the recipient to want them to receive something good, and b) actually have some sense about who the recipient is as a person in order to know what they'd like. Neither of those attributes apply to narcissists of course.

So the chances are very low that the gift will be anything you'd want even for its own sake. And still less do you need the reminder of her in your life.

So what do you do? Send it back or what?

I suggest that you do not send it back. To do so is communication of a kind, and as we said already, No-Contact means No Communication.

The ideal thing is to just donate it, still wrapped, to a local charity shop / thrift store.

And of course, you then do not acknowledge to your narcissistic mother that the gift arrived, or thank them for it. As far as she knows, it is lost in the void.

Likewise, when you are No-Contact, you do not send your

mother any gifts, no matter the importance of her milestones or occasions. She is a stranger to you now, and there are eight billion people on the planet whose special occasions you do not acknowledge and that's okay.

12.7.5: She has a crisis

Don't be surprised if, not long after you go No-Contact, your mother has a major crisis. And of course this major crisis necessitates you getting in touch with her. What *are* the odds?

This crisis could be a medical emergency, or a problem with her house, or a financial issue.

In truth, it might not even be a real crisis at all. It could be something she is making up, or exaggerating, or has caused to be worse than it otherwise would be, all to try to get your attention.

Whatever flavour of crisis it is, she will do her best to make sure you know about it. And of course you will feel pulled to get sucked in to help her with it. This is partly because you're a kind and compassionate person (which I know because, if you were not, you'd have gone No-Contact without a care in the world and wouldn't even be reading this book). And secondly because she taught you from the moment of your birth that you were responsible for her well-being and happiness, and that belief is ingrained deeply.

I invite you to remember that you were driven to going No-Contact by years of abuse, that you have not chosen this route, but she has made it necessary by her refusal to change, and so all of this is on her.

I invite you to recall that No-Contact is about severing all ties with her and all responsibility for her, and her having a crisis doesn't change that. I note that during anyone's life there will be crises of various forms, and that part of going No-Contact is acknowledging that these things will happen to her without you.

She might try to make you think, or you might tell yourself, that you are the only one who can help with this crisis. This might even be true to an extent: it wouldn't surprise me if she has engineered things all along so that you are responsible for her.

Even so, I offer you to give yourself permission not to respond. There must be another solution. What would she do if you were living abroad? Or if you were no longer alive? Let her do that.

Or, if you absolutely must sort out the problem, try to do it from a safe distance. Organise the ambulance, the medical appointment, the roof-repairer, etc., all without contact with her (or the minimum possible).

If you go rushing back to her if she has a crisis, you are teaching her that all she has to do to get you back is to have a crisis, and guess what she's going to do going forward?

Are you not a very bad and evil person to ignore someone who's having a crisis? I think not. All over the world people are having crises every single day and we don't help with those, simply because they are not our responsibility. And I argue that your mother's consistent hellish abuse makes this not your responsibility. If she had wanted a more present daughter, she should have treated you better. Your absence is nothing more or less than consequences, and you are not obliged to protect her from those, especially not at such a high cost to yourself.

12.7.6: She threatens suicide

This, unfortunately, is an all too common response. Far from guaranteed, but far from rare either.

She might well try to blame you for her being suicidal: she's going to kill herself because her life has no meaning without you. The terror and guilt you feel about this is overwhelming.

How do you deal with this?

First of all, we have to acknowledge that this is a very difficult situation. Let's pick our way carefully through it.

First, we need to remind ourselves that this situation is of *her* making. She is upset about a situation that she caused, and one that she could change if only *she* would change, but she chooses not to. This is down to her, not to you. You are only responding to her bad treatment of you. It's not as if you flounced off on some kind of whim.

Second, let's acknowledge that threatening suicide as a way of making you come back to her is the lowest form of manipulation. The fact that she would do that shows just how toxic she is and how right you are to remove yourself.

The third thing is that she is an adult who is legally *compos mentis*, i.e. she is in her whole mind (and if she is not, she needs to be in the care of the authorities), and has the right to make any decisions she chooses. And if that is suicide, so be it.

Does this sound harsh? I don't mean it to be. It is, rather, honouring her right as an independent adult to make her own decisions. And it is acknowledging that you, as an independent adult, equally have the right to make your own decisions and your decision is to cut off contact with her.

You are no less entitled to make decisions for your own life than she is.

Having said all that, if she threatens suicide, you need to take it very seriously.

If she is genuine about committing suicide, then she needs help, and if she is not, then she needs to have her bluff called.

But, this does *not* mean you need to drop everything and rush to her side. You can help her/call her bluff from a safe distance.

If she threatens it in the moment, then call an ambulance for her. If she is threatening it less specifically, e.g. saying she is suicidal in general, then inform everyone who needs to know: her partner, her doctor, her pastor, etc. Write to them rather than a phone call (or both), so they know to take it seriously.

And then, it will be what it will be. Regardless, it is not your responsibility.

What if she does commit suicide after all?

It is still not your responsibility. She was an adult who made her decision.

And truly, if you do not dare to cut contact in case she commits suicide, you are truly trapped, and she is being beyond abusive.

Only you can decide what decision you will make here, but I urge you to really ask yourself if it is fair for her to impose this dilemma on you. And if it is not, whether you need to be bound by it.

12.7.7: She stalks you

Your Narcissistic Mother might refuse to take your No-Contact letter for an answer, and start stalking you. Turning up at your house, constantly knocking on your door, constantly phoning you, turning up at work, contacting your employers, turning up at church and so on.

Don't mistake this as being a measure of how much she values you. As we said before, she is just missing her chew-toy. Also, she is possibly affronted and furious that you would dare to reject her, and is looking to remedy that situation.

In the first instance, just ignore her. She might well get the hint. But be sure to note every contact she makes in case you need to take it further.

And if she doesn't get the hint, do take it further. Take legal advice, and get yourself a restraining order. This is another reason to have written a No-Contact letter rather than just ghosting her, as then you already have proof that you told her to leave you alone.

It might seem extreme to invoke legal remedies, but she is the one who is being extreme by stalking you. You have the full right to protect yourself.

If you ignore her and she keeps trying to contact you, you might be tempted to break No-Contact long enough to tell her that you are serious about No-Contact, and to leave you alone. However, as Gavin de Becker says in his amazing book *The Gift Of Fear*, doing this only teaches her that if she contacts you often enough, she will get a response. So, apart from police or legal steps, you do not respond directly to her.

13
FLYING MONKEYS

13.1: All about Flying Monkeys

Flying Monkeys is the term used for the people who come to you and plead with you to go back to your mother.

We spoke of all the different ways your mother might react when you go No-Contact. If she just shrugs and carries on with her life, then most likely you won't have any problem with Flying Monkeys.

But if she wants to win you back because she is missing her Narcissistic Supply, and she either cannot or will not contact you directly, then she might well send Flying Monkeys to you. *Go and put some sense into her head*, she might say.

Or, the Flying Monkeys might come on their own initiative because your mother is giving them such grief about your absence.

Perhaps your mother is enjoying the drama of your 'betrayal', and all the attention it brings her. And no doubt she is genuinely hurting (remember: the cat that got the mouse confiscated is also genuinely hurting), and as narcissistic mothers never quite mastered stoicism or suffering bravely, she is inflicting that hurt onto others around her. Added to this her need to smear you and blame you and tell everyone how awful you are.

And so, you may be sure that everyone around her hears *ALL* about it. And so the Flying Monkey might feel pressured to do something about it even if your mother doesn't explicitly ask them to contact you.

There is another possible factor too: If you were the scapegoat, your narcissistic mother will have to find someone else to take that role, and you may be sure the new scapegoat won't like it and will want to remedy that situation as soon as possible, and get you back in place to take the abuse they are currently suffering.

So, for a variety of reasons, the people around your narcissistic mother will experience stress and trauma because of you going No-Contact, and they'll want to stop that stress and trauma, and so their solution will be to come to you and try to persuade you to go back to your mother.

The Flying Monkey will most likely be someone close to both you and your mother: close enough to your mother that they are in the blast zone of her meltdown, and close enough to you that they have access to you. And so it will probably be someone you love and whose good opinion you value, such as a sibling, an aunt, or your father, which makes it even more difficult to deal with.

We discuss below the various things they might say, and options for how you respond to them. In a way, though, these suggested responses are not for the Flying Monkeys at all, but for you. The Flying Monkey can sound like she's making a good argument, and I share the responses so you can see through them and realise they're not valid reasons to go back to your mother.

The ideal is to say as little as possible, in fact, and we discuss that next.

You don't have to entertain this discussion

Before we discuss what the Flying Monkeys might say and how you might respond, be aware that you do not have to have this discussion at all. You need to know that you never have to be part of any conversation you don't want to be part of. Conversation is like sex: both parties have to consent.

As soon as you realise that the Flying Monkey is there to

argue your mother's case you can say, calmly, but firmly, 'I am not going to discuss Mom with you. Let's talk about something else.' And then change the subject to something you are happy to talk about, e.g., 'How is Jan getting on in her new job?'

Now, this Flying Monkey is on a mission and most likely will not be so easily diverted, so you will have to set strict boundaries. I do go into the techniques of boundary-setting in my book *Become A Boundaries Badass*, and you can find out about it at donm.info/babb, and you might find that useful. For now though just know this:

If/when they persist, you set a firm boundary: 'I am not going to discuss Mom with you. We'll need to talk about something else or I'm going to have to leave/hang up.'

And then, if/when they still persist, you do what you said you would: either leave or hang up or otherwise end the conversation.

Now, they will not be happy with this, needless to say. But your freedom comes from allowing them to be unhappy. The only other option is for you to be involved in a conversation you don't want, and that would make you unhappy. So if one of you has to be unhappy, it doesn't have to be you.

This might feel rude, but remember how we spoke before about giving yourself permission to be appropriately rude. If someone is imposing on you, *they* have broken the social contract first.

The bad news is that it's very possible that they will cut off contact with you too, after this. But you knew this was a possibility when you made the No-Contact decision.

You can, in theory, offer to stay in a relationship with them independent of your mother, but in practice this is unlikely to be possible. Your mother will not tolerate it as she would feel that it was a betrayal of her. And the Flying Monkey will feel caught in the middle (which, in a way, they are).

And even though you're not making them choose between your mother and you, your mother certainly will. And they most likely will choose your mother for various reasons: one is that, as we said, they're no doubt still caught in your mother's toxic web, and another of which is that your mother is far more vicious than you are and would extract a high price for the Flying Monkey choosing you.

Add to which, if they side with you and your mother then rejects them accordingly, they might well lose all the rest of the extended family too. So the pull is strong for them to keep your mother sweet, and if they have to reject you in the process, that is just collateral damage. They may regret it of course, but they may well feel they have no option.

Bear in mind too, the old adage that if you're explaining, you're losing. If you start explaining yourself to the Flying Monkey, you are leaving the door open for her to argue you out of your position, so you might well decide the best option is not to discuss it at all.

Should you tell the Flying Monkeys about Narcissistic Personality Disorder?

What about sharing the information about Narcissistic Personality Disorder with the Flying Monkeys? You might think that if you do that they will realise the truth about your mother, and acknowledge why you had to go No-Contact.

Unfortunately, this is unlikely to work.

Instead, they could get very protective of your mother and turn on you in defence of her. Don't forget how long and difficult a journey it took you to get to this point. The Flying Monkey hasn't even begun that journey, most likely, because if they had, they wouldn't be so quick to be a Flying Monkey.

In addition, there is a psychological trait, which all us humans are prone to, called the Sunk Cost Fallacy. This means that if we have invested hugely in something, even if it hasn't worked out as we hoped, we find it hard to let it go simply because we have invested so much and need/want to have that investment pay off. We don't want to just write it off. And the Flying Monkey is clearly super-invested in the dynamic since they are arguing your mother's case.

So I would not recommend just bluntly telling them about Narcissistic Personality Disorder.

Having said that, you could say something very careful and very tentative to see how the Flying Monkey reacts. Something like a mild 'I didn't do it on a whim. There were reasons.'

If they get all huffy and defensive, your work here is done; there is nothing to discuss any more.

However, if they ask with curiosity and genuine interest (and maybe even a tiny bit of hope too) about your reasons, you can progress the conversation by saying something mild like, 'I find her very difficult.' And then see how they react to that. Try and get them to commit a little bit before saying any more after that, for example, asking them if they find her at all difficult.

In this way, in baby steps, each of you taking a step towards the truth in turn, you might be able to lead the Flying Monkey to a full discussion.

However, I share this possibility only for the sake of completeness as I do not expect that this will happen. Again, if they're her Flying Monkey, they're all in.

Are the Flying Monkeys victims, or co-perpetrators?

Both, I would say.

The fact is that a narcissistic mother creates a whole toxic dynamic around her, and all the family members are caught up in it. You know this well: you were caught up in it too, to the extent that you searched for and found this resource to help you free yourself. And look at how many steps we had to take in this resource to get you to the stage of walking away. It's not easy. And the Flying Monkey might well not even be asking the questions yet, never mind having any answers.

I think that anybody who is in the orbit of a narcissist is a victim of hers. They must be, because she does not have equals, or partners, or friends. She has only those who toe the line.

But if they start trying to get you to come back to your mother, they are also co-perpetrators. They are trying to keep you trapped in the dysfunction. I have no doubt that they don't see it like that, but that's what it is all the same.

13.2: The sort of things they say

So, you can totally refuse to discuss your mother or your No-Contact decision with the Flying Monkey. But just in case you do decide to listen to them, we'll explore next the sort of things they say, and how you might respond. And also, and most importantly: to show how they are wrong in what they say no matter how logical it might seem on the surface.

'How could you do this to your own mother?'
This is the equivalent of the narcissistic mother's snapping fingers. It's designed to make you ashamed of going No-Contact, to deny you the right to make your own decisions. It's a hugely disrespectful thing to say in that it assumes the speaker has to right to talk down to you, to scold you.

And there's an implication inherent in this too, in that you are doing this *to* your mother, rather than doing this *for* you. It's assuming that you are mistreating your mother. And so it puts you on the back foot to start with.

Again, you have no obligation to even be in this conversation, but just in case you want to, you have a few options for a response.

You could say, as I said above, that you not doing it *to* her, but rather *for* your own well-being, that you are sorry she is upset, but it doesn't change the reality.

You could say, if this is true, that you tried to fix things but she wouldn't work with you, and so this is your only remaining option. However, this allows the Flying Monkey to argue that your mother *did* work with you, or will, or could, and that is a discussion that has no profitable end.

Your response then is, 'She had her chance, and did not, and that is the end of it.'

'She's so sad; she's crying all the time.'

This one is designed to make you feel guilty, and I imagine that it will indeed succeed in its aim.

I remind you that guilt, like all emotions, is a messenger from your beliefs, and that sometimes your beliefs can be wrong. And any belief that tells you that you need to stay in touch with an abuser has got to be a wrong belief.

So you can feel the guilt – you have to, as if it comes it is there anyway – but you don't have to believe it. And you certainly don't have to act on it.

The implication in the statement about your Narcissistic Mother being sad – or it might not even be an implication as the Flying Monkey might say it directly – is that you have the power to stop the sadness, if only you'd come back. And that might well be true, but it doesn't take into account that by doing that you're walking into an abusive situation again.

And again, if you open the discussion it can't really end well, but if you want you could say something like, 'That's not going to happen.' And then shut down the conversation by saying, 'Now, let's talk about something else.'

Or you can use fauxpologies again: 'I'm sorry she's sad.'

'That's just how she is'/'Ahh you know what she's like'

This seems to be a favourite phrase of Flying Monkeys.

This statement acknowledges that she is difficult, but implies that you have to put up with it.

Nope!

The Flying Monkey is right about one thing: The fact is that yes, this is how she is. You know this already.

But that's the problem! This is why you have removed yourself from her: because this is how she is and she won't change.

The subtext here is that, because this is just the way your mother is, you should just put up with whatever behaviour she dishes out. This is not a valid argument!

Note especially the use of the word *'just'*. That word is doing a lot of heavy lifting here. It is used to dismiss the issue. It is almost saying that the way she is is just a fact of life, like weather patterns, and like weather patterns we just have to put up with them. It's dismissing the weight and enormity of how she is. This is the sort of statement that seems to imply the way she is is just some kind of foibles or irritating patterns.

Nope, the way she is is downright and consistently abusive.

In fact, I think it's fair to draw the opposite conclusion from 'just the way she is'. If this is the way she is (no 'just'), then she's not going to change, so your only options are to continue to put up with bad treatment or to remove yourself from the situation, and you have decided to honour yourself enough to refuse to endure bad treatment.

How much of this you say to the Flying Monkey is of

course up to you, but at least let you be aware of how flawed an argument it is.

'I understand – I find her difficult too'

This statement is a twin to the previous one, in that it acknowledges that your mother is difficult, but has the subtext that you have to endure her treatment of you regardless. The Flying Monkey is in effect saying, 'I find her difficult too, but I put up with her, so why can't you?'

Again, don't fall for this one. We don't need consensus in order to free ourselves from abuse.

If you think it's worthwhile, you could ask the Flying Monkey what she finds difficult about your mother, and then give a sympathetic uh-uh and see where the conversation goes. They might be dying to talk about how your mother stresses them.

'Be the bigger person'

This is another one of the Flying Monkeys' *Greatest Hits*: 'Yes, I know she's being unreasonable. But you know what she's like. So, come on, be the bigger person here.'

Be the bigger person. Right.

Be the bigger person, with the implication that if you hold your position then you're a small person, a narrow, bigoted, petty person.

Put like that, it's hard to refute.

But again, it's a flawed argument.

In a way that the Flying Monkey most likely will not appreciate, you are already being the bigger person. You are being the one who is adult enough (i.e. big enough) to refuse to put up with abuse. You are the one being mature enough to step outside dysfunction and manipulation, to stop playing toxic games.

And that even without that, you have no obligation to be the bigger person. In healthy relationships people are equally big.

That 'being the bigger person' is just a euphemism for 'let her continue to treat her exactly as she wishes while you roll over and take it,' and that you have no obligation whatsoever do that.

And that the Flying Monkey is being disingenuous to dress that up as some kind of virtue. And even more disingenuous to dress it up in their concern for your mother when it is most likely about their own wish to no longer experience the fallout of your absence.

'Can you not just forgive her?'

This is another *Just get over it*, disguised as something high and morally better.

To forgive someone does not mean you have to continue to put up with abuse. You can forgive (if you choose) from a safe distance. And forgiveness normally comes after genuine apologies, and your mother hasn't even acknowledged any wrongdoing let alone promising to change.

To the Flying Monkey you could say (if it was true and if you wanted to say it): 'I do forgive her.'

And they'll say, 'Great, so you can get in touch with her again!'

And then they've given away their agenda.

In this case you need only say, 'I am forgiving her without contacting her again.'

'You're just bearing a grudge'

This is the counterpoint to the forgiveness card. This is saying that all that is wrong is that you are bearing a grudge. It says nothing about your mother's behaviour or your need to protect yourself from her.

I hope it is clear how toxic and unfair this argument is, and how you have zero obligation to entertain it.

Plus, the arrogance of this statement to assume they know what's going on in your mind!

In a way this can be a manifestation of the Flying Monkey's need to resolve contradictory facts. On the one hand they are still in your mother's web, and must continue to believe in her goodness. On the other hand there is the reality that you have left the relationship. How can both those statements be true? The only logical result is that you are bearing a grudge. It does make sense when you think of it like that.

But it's still wrong.

'Do it for me?'

'It' of course being to get back in touch with your mother.

This can be a very hard one to resist, as you presumably want to please this person and they are asking you for a favour.

But again, they are putting unfair pressure on you. They are trying to manipulate you by making your relationship with your mother something that impacts on them. It is, of course, but they should be sorting that out with your mother rather than asking you to solve the problem.

In effect they are saying, 'Please put up with abuse for my sake.'

'She is so upset that she's suicidal'

We spoke earlier about what to do if your mother threatens suicide directly to you, and the same advice applies if it's the Flying Monkey saying she's at risk: tell the Flying Monkey to contact your mother's doctor/partner/pastor immediately and make them aware of this. Now that you have this information, you might also choose to contact these people directly too.

But also, be very clear that just because your mother is threatening suicide does not mean you have to go back to her. If you do, you are trapped forever, because she knows she can make that threat any time and it will always work.

14
WHAT IF YOU
MEET HER?

14.1: What if you meet her by chance?

Depending on how near you live to your mother, there is a possibility you might bump into her someday, by pure chance rather than her stalking you.

How will you manage that?

I do strongly urge you to decide ahead of time what you will do (and this text is to help you decide that), so that you can park that decision, so to speak, secure in the knowledge that it is there, and that you don't have to stress or fret every time you are out and about in case you meet her.

I think you would be wise to decide that you will not stop to speak to her, for all the reasons we have spent this whole resource discussing. You have closed the door and don't need to open it again.

One option therefore is a polite brief nod while you don't break stride and keep walking. To my mind this is a reasonable compromise between engaging with her and totally ignoring her. See how that sits with you as an option. The trouble is that she might see this as encouragement to open engagement with you again. The old give-her-an-inch-and-she'll-take-a-mile thing.

Or, just blank her completely. Yes, you are allowed to do this. She is just someone that you used to know, remember? Do you acknowledge all the strangers? Yes, she will find it rude, but that's okay. Yes, she may well complain to everyone about how awful you are, and that's okay too. As we've already discussed, she is never going to understand why you've gone No-Contact, and will always have her narrative, and your freedom and power lie in letting that be okay. Also, if you have built your wall securely, you won't hear back what she says so it will not impact on you.

What if she tries to speak to you though? What do you do?

Truly, there will be no value in having this conversation, so you could decide to say something very brief like, 'Stop now,' or hold up your hand in the *stop now* signal, and move on.

If she follows you, you could try telling her,'Stop following me,' but what if she doesn't? In this case, you could always just ignore her. That is always in your power. Just keep walking/ doing what you were doing, and let her trot along after you begging you to speak to her or whatever. I know this will take a lot of doing, but it is very effective. And of course, being ignored is narcissists' kryptonite, so by merely protecting yourself you are doing the thing she hates most.

If she grabs you or assaults you then of course this whole situation is escalated, and I would remove yourself in whatever way you can, and, if you choose, speak to the police about it.

Say you do decide to stop and speak to her, I would reiterate the advice I gave about if you were willing to engage if she turned up at your door: i.e. hear her out rather than engaging with her. She will not be engaging in good faith, trying to fix the situation.

But you are probably better off not even going this far. Otherwise the conversation could go something like:

Her: Why won't you talk to me.
You: As I said in the No-Contact letter, the relationship is toxic/abusive.
Her: In what way?
You: Well one example would be the time you did X.

Her: I didn't do X/you overreacted about X/ you can't take
a joke about X.

> Exercise 18: Decide what you'll do if you do meet her,
> and practise your action until it's natural.

14.2: What if you are invited to the same occasion?

What if you do still have family or friends in common with
your Narcissistic Mother, and one of those invites you to a
party or celebration, but your mother will be there too?

To be honest, if I were in that situation I would very
seriously consider not going. Yes, this is unfair, and sad, and
I do not minimise that one bit. You should be able to go to
these occasions.

However, it could well be stressful for you because you will
be spending hours in the same location as your mother with
huge potential for her to create drama with you and cause you
trauma. And it could also be very unfair on the hosts because
your mother could very well create drama at what should be
their occasion. You can trust yourself to be mature and calm
and respectful, but you cannot trust your mother to be like that.

So, the simplest – if not the easiest – solution is to
gratefully and politely decline.

If you do go to the occasion, if there are enough people
there, just try to avoid your mother. Maybe give her a polite
smile and bland, 'nice to see you', if it would cause more
trouble to ignore her.

If she does approach you and talk to you, you can just be polite and bland, 'Doesn't the bride look beautiful?'

Above all, I strongly suggest, this is not the time or place to discuss why you went No-Contact, or anything important. In truth, I hope you realise now that there is never a time or place now; she missed her chance. But someone else's special occasion is definitely not one!

15
CHECKING IN AGAIN

So, we are nearly at the end of this journey together, and so I'm taking this opportunity to check in with you again to see how you feel now about going No-Contact.

I invite you to make that decision now, if you have not already done so.

Are you happy to go No-Contact, and feel comfortable that you know how to do so?

Or are you willing to stay in Contact, now that you know what No-Contact involves?

Either way I hope you have peace about your decision.

If you are not in that place of clarity, then I suggest you try some of the resources you've learned: Tapping, Freewriting, and Committee Meetings to see what is blocking you (if you don't know already) and/or The Tapping Tree to chase your thoughts and beliefs to discover them.

If you do decide to stay in Contact, I do invite you to check out my book, *Become A Boundaries Badass*, at donm.info/babb, to help you manage your mother better. And, even if you do go No-Contact, this book could help you too as you will need to learn how to set boundaries with other people after a lifetime of being taught not to.

16
WHAT NEXT?

16.1: What next in your own life?

You might well experience vivid dreams featuring your mother / parents – nightmares, even – in the first while after going No-Contact. I certainly did, and I've heard the same from other DONMs. In these dreams we were shouting at our Narcissistic Mother, or maybe even hitting her. It wasn't a bit nice. But in retrospect I think it was about us claiming our power, the power we had never had. And nobody got hurt in real life, and the dreams faded in time, after they had done their job maybe.

So if this happens to you it seems to me that this is nothing to worry about, as long as the dreams pass.

After going No-Contact we can experience deep grief. This is completely understandable. There is a huge loss here, or – perhaps more accurately – the acknowledgment of the loss you always had but never let yourself accept until now.

And, even more painfully, it's a loss without cultural and societal support. When other women lose their mothers, it is to death rather than this severing we call No-Contact, and there are funerals, and societal support, and closure and people understand if you're weepy and so on.

We DONMs have none of those, which can make it worse as it's such a private grief and a secret loss and an unsupported journey.

Grief is very simple, but not a bit easy. It's less a problem to be solved than a situation to be endured and processed. I do offer you two of the resources that are available via the Resources page: Comfort tapping and the grief script.

But also, allow yourself to feel the grief. Don't feel that you shouldn't feel grief because a) she was a horrible mother and/or b) you chose this, or whatever other narrative you tell yourself.

This loss was necessary, yes, but it is still real.

The sad reality is that our own partner, or our adult children, or our friends, often do not understand just how toxic our narcissistic mother is. They might well say, and mean, 'But she's always nice to me.'

And you know, she might well be. Narcissists can be very clever in who they reserve their nastiness for, even going so far as to only abuse you in private, or in hidden coded ways that others won't notice.

Or they might say, 'But she's your mother, of course she loves you.'

This is a tough one for sure, and yet again there are no good options, just your choice of bad options.

You can try to explain to them exactly how narcissists are. If they are on your team, they should at least listen. And if they still don't get it (and in fairness, it is difficult to get your head around narcissism if you have never experienced it), they should still respect your decision, and agree to support you even if they don't agree with your decision.

One consequence of going No-Contact with a narcissistic mother is that it gives you space to look at your other relationships, even despite yourself, and that can lead to realising that other relationships are toxic, and those relationships ending too. This can be very painful, but it is always for the best as you lose the toxic people and make room for healthy relationships. My own marriage ended after I went No-Contact. Not that my ex was in any way toxic or abusive, but the marriage wasn't right for either of us, and with the space No-Contact gave, we were able to see that.

Quite apart from those people who leave you, DONMs often find that once they go No-Contact, they start to notice toxicity in their other existing relationships. This, understandably, will be both confusing and heartbreaking.

Confusing because, hang on, does this mean *everyone* is toxic? Or could it all be you: you're the common denominator here after all?

And do you have to cut them off too? Are you doomed to loneliness?

First of all, take deep breaths. No, it is not you, not in the way you're worried about anyway. What has happened is that, trained as you were by your mother, you were a magnet for other narcissists and toxic people. That makes sense, right?

And of course, no you don't have to cut them off. You don't have to do anything you don't want to do.

But I offer you that you would *want* to cut them off. You have made the hardest decision of them all: to cut off your own mother because she was too toxic. Why would you let any less-important people stay in your life if they mistreat you?

But yet it might be too much loss. I get that. That's the heart-breaking bit and there's no way to soften that. It hurts. It really really hurts.

However, I invite you think of this more like a house-cleaning. Decluttering maybe. And what will be left will be the space to create good and healthy relationships.

Having said that, you don't have to do anything yet either. You can work on your own timetable. Don't feel pressured to make any other decisions until and unless you are ready.

But, you might worry, will this mean you're left totally alone?

It might, at least temporarily.

But I offer you to consider that that could be okay. That you could be your own best friend and your own company.

Now, I know this is easier to say than to do. We're tribal beings as we discussed already, and we need other people. So this is a bit of a conflict; I do understand that.

I stand by what I'm saying, however. Being alone is far far from the worst thing. Being in toxic and abusive relationships is the worst thing. And the more you are able/comfortable/willing to be alone, the less you will need to endure toxic relationships.[5]

And being alone will give you the space to find other good people.

Or not. Ten years after my own marriage ended, I have not found another partner. But the thing is: that's okay! I have made – and continue to make – a really satisfying and wonderful life without that. If I do meet anyone else, it will be a bonus in an already good life, not a necessary component. And being willing to be alone has given me the strength to say no to relationships that would not be good for me. To refuse to settle. In that lies power, and that is what I offer for you to consider, both with regard to romantic relationships and friendships.

The less needy you are, the more likely you are to attract healthy people to be in relationships with.

And speaking of finding good people, let's discuss that next.

When you feel ready, you might like to find your tribe so to speak. Depending on your stage of life, it might be easier or harder to find new friends, new people to be in your life, but it's important, especially if you have lost a lot of people after going No-Contact. One way to meet new people is through

[5]   Check out the Resources page for studies on the dangers of being lonely on the one hand, and the dangers of being in toxic abusive relationships on the other.

joining groups and clubs, and we will be discussing this in detail shortly, and why it's important in discovering who you are without your mother.

As much as is possible, be aware that any new friend would be lucky to have you in their lives as much as you'd be lucky to have them. I know it can be hard to value ourselves that way but the more you can do that, the better. You could even tap on it, using the issue statement, 'I don't feel I bring value to any friendship,' or any similar statement that sits well with you.

Or, invite the committee member(s) who think you are a burden rather than a gift to come and resolve that belief with you.

And if you do spend some lonely (or will we call it *alone?*) time, tap and/or freewrite to manage that loneliness, and take this opportunity to be your own best friend and enjoy your own company.

It can be terrifying to spend time alone, but once you face that terror, it can be wonderful as you come to meet yourself. After all, how can you expect others to want to spend time with you, if you do not want to do that?

Don't be tempted to settle by letting toxic people into your life. You are worth more than that. You have proven that you will set standards for how the people in your life treat you, and you never ever need to compromise on that.

One further note: be aware that after these trauma-bonded chaotic not-knowing-where-you-stand relationships, healthy relationships can feel boring. But that is the way it should be! Boring is just another word for stable, and happy. Living in war is more exciting than living in peace, but living in peace is the desired state. But we can get addicted to the chaos and the fear and the trauma, and the more we recognise this addiction the less power it has over us. You can also use EFT/Tapping to help free yourself from this dynamic.

But who will you be without her?

We can get very addicted to trying to win our mother's approval, and our lives can feel very empty if we are no longer striving for that.

Plus, in a way you won't really appreciate until things change, the dynamic with your narcissistic mother takes huge amounts of time, and emotional and psychological energy. Once that need is gone, you can feel very deflated and empty almost.

Also, we can subconsciously define ourselves by our relationship with her. Who then will we be if she is no longer in our lives?

The solution to this is: *PLAY.*

Often as adults we forget to play, or feel we don't have the time, or think we should have grown out of that by now. But play is essential to a happy life, and it's a great way to find out who we are. What we choose to do for play is a clue to our souls.

The rules for play are simple:

- You should enjoy it
- There should be zero pressure to create a result. Process not product. The play is an end unto itself. So, say you bake a cake, yes, you'll have a cake at the end of it, but you won't feel you have to enter competitions or set up a baking business.

So I invite you to think of ways you could play, and to commit to one play-session each week. What could your play include? The suggestions below are just to trigger ideas. If any of them make your heart sink, then they are not play for you.

Also, try to make it easy and low stakes and impossible to get wrong. If you have to practise loads, and go through a learning curve during which you find it tough: those things still have value, but they are not this play process.

- Painting/art (but just for the sake of it, no need to end up with something good)
- Storytelling/writing (likewise)
- Dancing, either by yourself in your kitchen, or more formally
- Singing, again either by yourself in your kitchen, or more formally
- Hiking
- Going to concerts/museums/art galleries
- Going to a sports game
- Joining a sports club
- Going to chi-chi markets
- A long chat with a good friend
- Bike rides
- A sport you like
- Baking
- Cooking a fancy meal
- Joining a drama group/taking acting lessons
- Or improvisation: the ultimate process of no pressure and being in the moment
- Swimming/kayaking/paddle boarding, or any water sport that appeals
- Coffee/tea in a new place
- Exploring a new town
- Being a tourist in your own town.

Also, know that for a while it'll feel strange to be your own person without reference to your mother, and just accept that feeling. It will pass as you start to fill your world with people and events which enrich you and fulfil you rather than drag you down.

16.2: What to say to others?

So, what do you say to other people about the fact that you are No-Contact? This is a big question, especially since we are going against Society's stories by cutting off our mothers.

There is no absolute answer to this, as the permutations are endless: your personality, your exact situation, your relationship with each of the other people, your desire or lack of it to explain, and so on. But let's see if we can tease out some guiding principles at least.

The first of those is to say as little as you can easily get away with. Most people aren't really asking; they're just making conversation. So, say you're at work and a colleague asks if you're going home for Thanksgiving or Christmas or whatever, you can just say casually and blandly something like, 'Oh, not this year, what about you?'

If it's a more complex situation: say the person is really asking, not just making conversation, you can choose how much or how little to say. Know that if they are probing or pushing, then they are being rude and nosy and you don't have to be polite back. I'm not saying to be proactively rude or nasty, of course, but you don't have to be pleasant either. So you could say simply, 'I don't want to discuss this. Now [insert change of subject here].'

Or, if you do want to speak your truth, you might like to have a set sentence learned off, something like: 'My mother is toxic and abusive so I have cut off contact with her for my mental health.'

And if you're willing to discuss it further, great – say they are genuinely interested, because don't forget that although Society plays the game of Happy Families, many many families are toxic and dysfunctional, for reasons of Narcissistic Personality Disorder or a myriad of other reasons, such as alcoholism. So maybe you admitting this truth can be a gift to them, opening the door for them to speak their own truth, to themselves and/or to you.

However, if they're being nosy and/or trying to catch you out or blame you for going against Society's narrative, then have a set phrase ready such as, 'It's not open for discussion.'

Know that you do not have to be a part of any conversation you don't want to be part of.

16.3: Second guessing yourself

Of course doubts will arise. That is the human condition anyway, and even more so for us DONMs who were taught to doubt ourselves and minimise the bad treatment. You might start second-guessing yourself as to whether you were right, or fair, or reasonable, to go No-Contact.

There are a few ways to manage this.

The first is to know that doubts are just a feeling, and you don't have to be steered by your feelings any longer. You can breathe through that feeling and know that it is here, and that is fine, but you are not going to act on it.

The second is to re-read your *Greatest Hits* document. This is information from Past-You as to why you wanted and needed to go No-Contact.

The third is to re-read the No-Holds-Barred No-Contact letter you wrote for yourself.

The fourth is to Freewrite a letter to yourself and explore the issue.

The fifth way is to call a committee meeting with the part of you that is second-guessing yourself, and discuss it with them.

And the sixth is to use EFT/Tapping, using the Tapping

Tree process where you follow all your thoughts without judgement or expectation, and that will give you resolution.

The resolution might be that you *will* contact her again, and the next section deals with that.

You can always change your mind

As the heading says, you can always change your mind about going No-Contact, and get in touch again with your narcissistic mother. Sometimes our longing for our mother, and our hope that all can be redeemed, brings us back to her to try again. Sometimes we need to go back, even to go back a few times, before No-Contact 'takes' so to speak.

I have carefully constructed the flow of this resource to make this unlikely, because this is not the ideal situation. I want you to be strong in your decision when you make it. But the power always remains with you, and you always have the authority to make a different decision.

But she might not accept you back

However, just as you have your freedom to choose, so does your mother. She might be so angry with you that she refuses to let you come back. When you decide on going No-Contact, be very clear that this is something you risk.

Whether she accepts you back or not, a lot will depend on whether she is getting enough Narcissistic Supply from others, or whether she needs it from you, and on how much mileage she is getting from the drama of your departure.

And if she does accept you back, she will possibly extract her price

If she does accept you back, you may well have to grovel and apologise profusely first. She surely will not. You will have to accept the blame for everything.

Also, once contact is established, you may well have a honeymoon period where she is being nice, but as we said before, after a while she will almost certainly punish you with extra nastiness. She will have to punish you for daring to reject her at all, plus there is all the pent-up nastiness that she didn't get to dump on you during your break from her.

Of course, you can always go back to No-Contact, and repeat as often as needed until it finally takes. There is no shame in this: leaving one's own mother is surely one of the most difficult and complex actions anybody can take.

They say it takes women seven tries to leave an abusive partner – I couldn't find a source for this; it just seems to be repeated as a truism all over, but I can well believe it. And it could take DONMs seven times, or at least a number of times, to leave fully.

And that's okay!

There's no one right way to go No-Contact with your abusive mother. You will find your own way and that is the way that is right for you.

Dear Fellow-DONM, thank you so much for taking this journey with me. I hope that you are truly empowered now to be free from the toxic relationship that had you trapped. I would love to hear from you with comments and feedback at donm.info/Email

I invite you to go to donm.info/htgnc-resources to check out the various resources to go with this book. You do not need this, as everything needed is in this book, but the free resources are helpful, and the paid resources are nice-to-have if you choose.

I would be endlessly grateful if you could leave a review for this book, wherever you choose.

To date I have written three other books for daughters (and sons!) of Narcissistic Mothers. You can purchase print copies from my publisher's site donm.info/dltbooks or e-book versions at donm.info/shop.

And lastly, let's keep in touch! I invite you to sign up for my email series, The DONM Guidebook to Healing And Thriving. The subscribe link is donm.info/Guidebook.

Again, thank you so much for taking this journey with me.

Hugs to you,